Welcome

At 04.08 hours on the morning of 13 June 1944, two members of the Royal Observer Corps, on duty at Dymchurch in Kent, spotted the approach of an object spurting red flames from its rear and making a noise like 'a Model-T-Ford going up a hill'. The first V1 flying bomb, an example of what Hitler had called his Vergeltungswaffen or Vengeance weapons, to be released against Britain was rattling towards them.

The pilotless aircraft continued over the North Downs before it fell to earth with a loud explosion near Gravesend ten minutes later. Before there had been time to take stock of the situation, another V1 track was reported, which then turned westward and exploded just north of Cuckfield in Sussex. Two more quickly followed, with one dropping in London and the other close to Sevenoaks in Kent. It was the London bomb which caused the first doodlebug, or buzz-bomb, casualties in the UK.

Hitler's V weapon campaign reached a new intensity on 8 September 1944, when a V2 rocket slammed into the ground and exploded in Chiswick. With the V2, however, there was almost no chance of a warning being given, and the effects of their detonation in built-up areas were devastating.

By the time that the last flying-bombs and rockets fell in March 1945, approximately 18,000 people, mostly civilians, had been killed. It was only the huge multi-agency, inter-Allied response that had prevented even more casualties – and which, by chance, had also eliminated the threat of another of Hitler's V weapons, the V3 supergun.

From the very moment that Allied intelligence first warned of the existence of the V1 and V2, the full story of the development and operational deployment of these weapons, along with that of the V3, is explored here. The human and social cost, and how the threats were overcome or managed, are also revealed – as is how those involved in Hitler's terror campaign would go on to become an integral part of the post-war race to the moon.

John Grehan

John Grehan
Editor

ACKNOWLEDGMENT: The editorial team would like to thank Robert Mitchell for his unstinting help on the pictures.

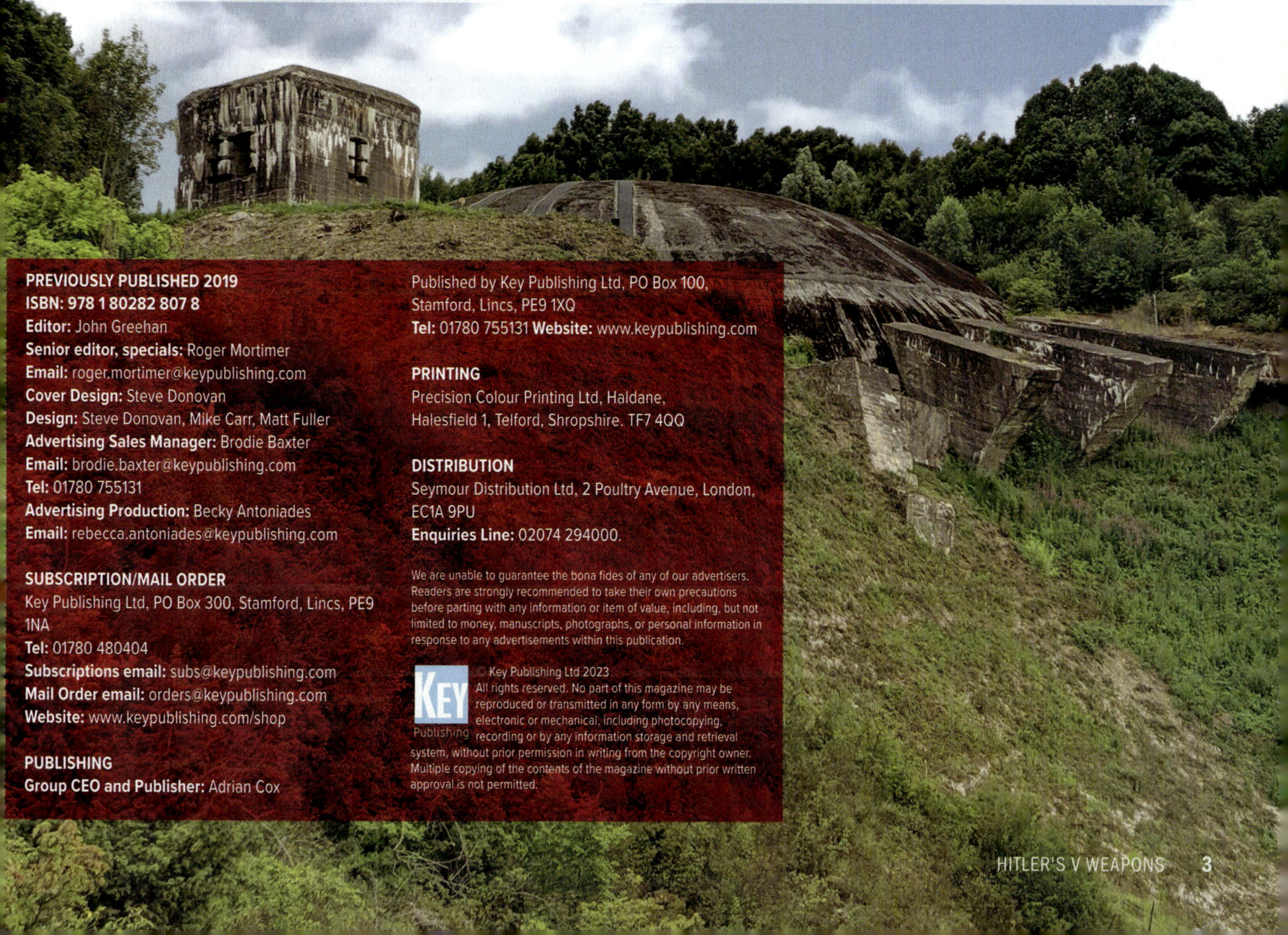

BELOW *The massive dome of the V2 site now known as La Coupole at Wizernes in northern France.* (HISTORIC MILITARY PRESS)

PREVIOUSLY PUBLISHED 2019
ISBN: 978 1 80282 807 8
Editor: John Greehan
Senior editor, specials: Roger Mortimer
Email: roger.mortimer@keypublishing.com
Cover Design: Steve Donovan
Design: Steve Donovan, Mike Carr, Matt Fuller
Advertising Sales Manager: Brodie Baxter
Email: brodie.baxter@keypublishing.com
Tel: 01780 755131
Advertising Production: Becky Antoniades
Email: rebecca.antoniades@keypublishing.com

SUBSCRIPTION/MAIL ORDER
Key Publishing Ltd, PO Box 300, Stamford, Lincs, PE9 1NA
Tel: 01780 480404
Subscriptions email: subs@keypublishing.com
Mail Order email: orders@keypublishing.com
Website: www.keypublishing.com/shop

PUBLISHING
Group CEO and Publisher: Adrian Cox

Published by Key Publishing Ltd, PO Box 100, Stamford, Lincs, PE9 1XQ
Tel: 01780 755131 **Website:** www.keypublishing.com

PRINTING
Precision Colour Printing Ltd, Haldane, Halesfield 1, Telford, Shropshire. TF7 4QQ

DISTRIBUTION
Seymour Distribution Ltd, 2 Poultry Avenue, London, EC1A 9PU
Enquiries Line: 02074 294000.

Contents

ABOVE LEFT *Allied troops inspect a captured V1 flying bomb that has been put on public display in Paris in 1944/1945.* (SAN DIEGO AIR & SPACE MUSEUM)

ABOVE *War correspondents examine the tail sections of V2 rockets lined up on a roadside near Nordhausen after the German surrender.* (NARA)

BELOW *The V1 flying bomb that caused the damage pictured here exploded in York Road, near Waterloo Station in London, at 09.36 hours on 23 June 1944. According to one account, it 'destroyed general railway offices, 2 air shafts [and] an 8-car train; 100 feet of track were damaged and 5 streets suffered severe blast damage across 400 yards square'.* (HISTORIC MILITARY PRESS)

Weapons of War

THE ROCKETS THAT ONE DAY WOULD TAKE MAN TO THE MOON HAD THEIR ORIGINS IN A MEANS OF MASS DESTRUCTION.

LEFT *A gathering of German rocket pioneers, members of the Verein für Raumschiffahrt, pictured in 1930. The Verein für Raumschiffahrt, or VfR, was a German amateur rocket association which existed prior to the Second World War, being wound up in 1934 through a lack of funds. The VfR's first successful test firing with liquid fuel, which lasted five minutes, was conducted by Max Valier on 25 January 1930. From left to right, this group comprises Rudolf Nebel, Frank Ritter, unidentified, Kurt Heinisch, unidentified, Hermann Oberth, unidentified, Klaus Riedel, Wernher von Braun, and a further unidentified individual.* (LIBRARY OF CONGRESS)

In October 1933, the recently installed Chancellor of Germany, Adolf Hitler, visited the Army Weapons Office testing facility at Kummersdorf (Heeresversuchsanstalt Kummersdorf-Gut), around sixteen miles south of Berlin. There he was shown experiments which were being conducted in relation to the development of rocket motors that were fuelled by oxygen and alcohol. Hitler was not impressed with what he saw, and the project, which had been running for more than a year, appeared to have little future.

It had been as early as 1930 when Generalmajor Carl Becker, the head of the German Army Weapons Office, invited thirty-five-year-old captain Walter Dornberger to head a special unit to explore the practicality of developing military rockets on a large scale. Rockets, however, had been used in warfare long before the twentieth century.

Tipu Sultan, for example, had fired rockets at troops of the British East India Company in 1792, after which William Congreve developed a military rocket for the Royal Artillery. Congreve had some success with his rockets with the Royal Horse Artillery at the Battle of the Nations in 1813 and Waterloo two years later. Though such rockets were fearsome weapons, they were highly inaccurate and almost as dangerous to those who fired them as they were to the enemy.

Nevertheless, in the early twentieth century, a device for measuring precise distances and elevation angles, was developed. This was followed by the pulse-duration method of long-range measurements and, in 1928, the introduction of gyroscope-based control, which was perhaps the most critical invention for the future of rocketry. All the building blocks were therefore in place for the development of accurate rocketry when Dornberger set up his new unit at Kummersdorf on 1 August 1932.

To lead the team at Kummersdorf, Dornberger selected Wernher von Braun who was, at the time, undertaking post-graduate studies in physics at the Friedrich-Wilhelm University of Berlin (von Braun was awarded his doctorate in 1934). Von Braun's team's first test rocket, which was known as Aggregate 1, was a small projectile less than 5 feet long and weighing only 330lb. The A1's engine produced 300lbs of thrust for sixteen seconds, but the first rocket blew up on the launch pad. It was also considered that the gyroscope fitted in the nose of this small craft would render it top-heavy and unstable in flight. It was the trials with the A1 which had so unimpressed Hitler in 1933.

The next weapon designed by von Braun's team – the A2 – was, by comparison with its predecessor, a marked success. With the incorporation of gyrostabilisers in its design, the rocket, powered by a new engine which produced 3,000lbs of thrust, soared to more than 7,000 feet. Such missiles could not be flown from Kummersdorf and the test-firing of the A2 took place on Borkum island in the North Sea, far from population centres and, more importantly, away from prying eyes. It was at Borkum on 19 and 20 December 1934, that two rockets climbed beyond 10,000 feet.

Peenemünde

Improvements continued to be made both in the facilities at Kummersdorf and in the rockets von Braun's team were producing and the next step forward was a correspondingly huge one. The A3 was 22 feet long and weighed 1,650lbs. It had narrow fins to help its stability in flight and incorporated a radio receiver which enabled the ground crew to shut down the engine when required. Despite the improvements at Kummersdorf, its proximity to Berlin meant that security at the site was difficult to ensure. A new site had to be found, and it was the island of Usedom in the Baltic, a remote place where Wernher von Braun's father used to go duck hunting, which was chosen – and,

more specifically, the Peenemünde peninsula. The advantages offered by this site were that access to the island could be easily controlled and that missiles could be fired safely into the Baltic Sea whilst monitoring equipment could be installed along the Baltic/Pomeranian coast.

On 2 April 1936, the Reich's Ministry of Aviation (Reichsluftfahrtministerium) paid 750,000 Reichsmarks to the local town of Wolgast for the whole northern peninsula of Usedom. The cost was shared between the German army (Heer) and the air force (Luftwaffe). The village of Peenemünde was evacuated and the Heer and the Luftwaffe worked together to build a state-of-the-art research, test and production facility far in advance of anything in any other country. A huge 30,000-kilowatt coal-fired power station was built, as well as a large liquid oxygen factory. Also planned was a supersonic wind tunnel

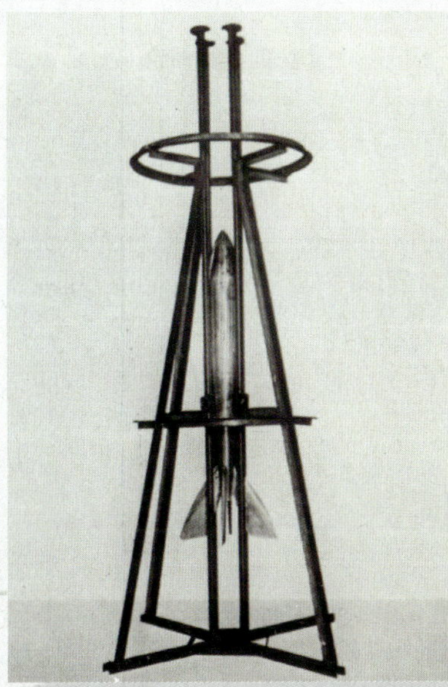

capable of the testing of the missiles at speeds of up to Mach 4.4 – 4.4 times the sound of speed.

A housing estate was built to accommodate the 1,200 or more technical and senior staff. To the south of this well-landscaped estate, at Karlshagen, were barracks intended for the German military, but which were turned into a labour camp to house some 1,500 male prisoners who were employed by the Luftwaffe. Further south still, at Trassenheide, was a concentration camp which held thousands of slave labourers in terrible conditions. Such was the scale of the Peenemünde site, it was still unfinished when war was declared in 1939.

The first of the 350 rocket scientists and engineers moved from Kummersdorf in April 1937, to continue work on the A3. But with the facilities at Peenemünde still under construction, the first trials of the new rocket were conducted at Greifswalder Oie, a small island in the Baltic Sea located east of Rügen on the German coast, in December of that year. The weather was awful and, in the strong winds that swept off the Baltic, the rocket was blown into a spin and crashed. All four attempts saw the rocket blown to the ground. Work on the A3 was abandoned, von Braun's team turning its attention to the next generation of rocket, the A4.

Hitler's disinterest

In 1938 the two services at Peenemünde separated with each developing their own sites on the peninsula. The Luftwaffe's Test Site ▶

was situated to the north and west of the peninsula while the Heer's Research Centre was located at Peenemünde Ost (East) where laboratories and production facilities were built. Nine rocket test stands were erected near the sandy coastline.

Also in 1938, Hitler disbanded the Reich Ministry of Defence (Reichswehrministerium) replacing it with the Oberkommando der Wehrmacht, the Armed Forces High Command, headed by Generalfeldmarschall Wilhelm

Keitel. It was this body which would oversee a massive increase in military spending, including the promise of greater support for the weapons programme at Peenemünde. But the problem was that Hitler remained unconvinced with the new technology and he was unwilling to release the enormous funding which was required to turn the rockets into military weapons. Dornberger believed that the rockets would give Germany the military muscle to dominate Europe and he needed to persuade the Führer to provide the necessary finance.

So, on 23 March 1939, Hitler was invited to Kummersdorf, where Dornberger explained the progress which had so far been achieved and of his hopes for the future of the rocket.

RIGHT *Another of the Verein für Raumschiffahrt's rocket design being filled up with liquid oxygen. It is possible that this rocket is one of the VfR's so-called Repulsor series which when successfully fired reached altitudes over 3,000 feet.* (LIBRARY OF CONGRESS)

LEFT *A picture of an A2 rocket with sectionalised fuselage, tanks and engine. The A2 was designed in 1934 by Wernher von Braun under a program at Kummersdorf that was headed by Walter Dornberger.* (LIBRARY OF CONGRESS)

RIGHT *An A2 engine undergoing static firing at Prüfstand, or Test Stand, No.1 at Kummersdorf. This stand was designed and constructed in 1932.* (LIBRARY OF CONGRESS)

BELOW *An area shot of the Heeres-versuchsanstalt Kummersdorf-Gut, or Army Weapons Office testing facility, at Kummersdorf – the countryside having become more wooded in the years since the end of the Second World War.*

Once again, Hitler was unmoved.

Work continued on the A4 and a smaller test version, the A5, though progress was not as rapid as the Aggregate team wished due to the financial constraints under which it strived. Hitler would, one day, regret his parsimony in this area.

Though still incomplete, the Peenemünde site was declared operational at the end of 1939. Command of the site was entrusted to Colonel Leo Zanssen. But, of course, Germany was already at war and every branch of the armed forces

was calling out for priority in terms of manpower and materials. It was entirely understandable that Hitler gave the conventional weapons – the ones that were actually in use on the battlefield – priority over something that offered future benefits, but which might never actually be needed. It would be another two years before Hitler would take an interest in the development of military rockets, but in 1939 the programme was far from advanced and the possibility of von Braun and his team producing anything useful for the German war effort appeared as distant as ever before.

Fluctuating fortunes

Undeterred, von Braun and his colleagues persevered with the A5, which was aerodynamically identical to the proposed A4 and included many of the latter's essential features, such as an inertia guidance system, radio-controlled engine cut-off and an engine powered by a similar alcohol/liquid oxygen mix. The first airborne 'drop test' models of the A5 were delivered to Peenemünde in the spring of 1938. If these could be made to fly successfully then scaling-up to the A4 would be a simple geometric task.

The first attempt was undertaken in September the following year, the rocket being dropped from 20,000 feet by a Heinkel He 111. This first trial was to test the rocket's stability at high speed as it dropped to 3,000 feet before it was slowed down by its retarding parachute.

> *"Ground launches were then conducted at Greifswalder Oie, the rockets racing to more than 30,000 feet with just 45 seconds of thrust before their engines were shut down."*

Ground launches were then conducted at Greifswalder Oie, the rockets racing to more than 30,000 feet with just 45 seconds of thrust before their engines were shut down. They splashed down in the sea close to the island from where they were recovered. The Siemens-manufactured gyro-autopilot guidance system proved to be highly satisfactory as the A5 soared to heights in excess of 40,000 feet and distances of eleven miles along the Baltic. Such was

LEFT A fully assembled A2 rocket pictured at Test Stand No.1 at Kummersdorf. The rocket is being fuelled up with liquid oxygen prior to a static firing. (LIBRARY OF CONGRESS)

RIGHT An A3 rocket in Test Stand No.3 at Kummersdorf – this was the largest of the test stands at this location. The stand was mobile, being moved on rails. (LIBRARY OF CONGRESS)

RIGHT German rocket development continues. Here the engine of an A4 rocket, the V2, is being fired at Test Stand No.1 at Peenemünde. (LIBRARY OF CONGRESS)

BELOW A general view of Prüfstand, or Test Stand, No.1 at Peenemünde. This test stand played an important part in the development of the A4's engine and rocket propulsion. (LIBRARY OF CONGRESS)

the very evident success of the A5, von Braun considered it was time to move up to the A4: 'What we had successfully done with the A5 must be equally valid, in improved form, for the A4 … I could see our goal clearly and the way that led to it. I now knew that we should succeed in creating a weapon with a far greater range than any artillery.'

Dornberger's aim was to build a massive rocket, capable of carrying a large warhead over long distances with considerable accuracy, but which could be transported on existing roads and railways on the continent. This would see the A4 measuring 46 feet in length with a diameter of 5 feet, and a weight of 9 tons with fuel onboard, which would carry a one-ton warhead of amatol explosive. Its engine, powered by ethanol/water and liquid oxygen, would deliver 55,000lbs to 66,000lbs of thrust for 65 seconds.

The Aggregate team had come a long way from its early efforts. But

those efforts were almost thwarted when, in 1940, France was defeated and the British Expeditionary Force was driven off the continent in a matter of weeks. With Dornberger predicting that the A4 would not be coming off the production lines until 1943, it appeared that the war would be won long before that date. Funding for the rocket programme was reduced. The defeat of the Luftwaffe in the Battle of Britain, however, concentrated minds once more and funding for the project was restored.

Into space

For von Braun and his team, the culminating moment of all their efforts came on 3 October 1942, with the first full-scale launching of the A4 at Peenemünde. Shortly after noon all was ready for the great moment. As Dornberger admitted, if the rocket failed, he would not be able to justify the huge consumption of resources that were being devoted to the programme. The tide of war had changed perceptibly during the intervening years and unless the rocket could realistically contribute significantly to the pursuance of ▶

the war, those resources must be diverted into the manufacture of tanks or aircraft.

The tension was palpable, as the seconds of the final minute were counted down. Then, 'Ignition!'. After about a second, the gleaming missile rose vertically from the deep green of the forest to the bright blue of the sky. Supersonic speed was achieved in moments, and when the red flame of the engine cut out, the rocket was racing into the distance at more than 3,000mph.

'I couldn't speak for a moment; my emotion was too great,' Dornberger was to relate. 'I could see that Colonel Zanssen was in the same state. He was standing there laughing. His eyes were moist. He stretched out his hands to me. I grasped them. Then our emotions ran away with us. We yelled and embraced each other like excited boys … Everyone was shouting, laughing, leaping dancing and shaking hands.'

The A4 reached a height of almost sixty miles. For the first time in human history, a man-made object had left earth and entered space. Once emotions had settled, Dornberger gave a speech to the gathered crowd of scientists and technicians: 'This third day of October 1942, is the first of a new era in transportation, that of space travel.' But as Dornberger was to remind his team: 'The development of possibilities we cannot yet envisage will be a peacetime task … So long as the war lasts, out most urgent task can only be the rapid perfection of the rocket as a weapon.'[1]

On 22 December 1942, Hitler, somewhat reluctantly, signed the order for mass production of what would become known as the *Vergeltungswaffen* (or Vengeance weapon) 2 – the soon to be feared V2.

The flying bomb

While the Heer was progressing satisfactorily, if slowly, with its rockets, nearby at Peenemünde West the Luftwaffe was developing its own unmanned missile. The Luftwaffe's High Command had seen and heard the Army's rockets with considerable disquiet. It had complained to the Minister of Armaments and Munitions, Albert Speer, that the Army was 'sprouting wings' and that the 'Army alone would be bombing London' in the future.

Work by the Argus Motoren company on a remote-controlled aircraft which could carry a 1,000kg payload for some 300 miles had been presented to the Reichsluftfahrtministerium on 9 November 1939, but the idea was not adopted by the ministry and development of the weapon remained in civilian hands. An improved version of the pilotless aircraft was submitted to the Air Ministry in April 1940, but this too was rejected. It was not until the Argus Motoren company joined forces with the Fieseler aircraft company that the new design of a 'flying bomb' was adopted by the RLM, under the name Fi.103. The date was 28 April 1942. As with Dornberger's rocket, much time had been lost.

This flying bomb, the future V1, was far simpler in design than the A4 rocket. It was almost 27 feet long with a wingspan of 17.6 feet, and was driven by a pulse-jet engine, in

ABOVE *An A5 rocket is test-launched from a wooded area on Greifswalder Oie in 1942.* (CRITICAL PAST)

RIGHT *A veteran of the VfR, Kurt Heinisch (on the left), who appears in the early group photograph on page 6, pictured in the control room at Test Stand No.1 at Peenemünde.* (LIBRARY OF CONGRESS)

BELOW *A view of the island of Greifswalder Oie, which lies about 7.5 miles from Usedom. Between 1938 and 1942 the island was the scene of test launches of the A5, whilst twenty-eight V2s were launched vertically from there between 1943 and 1945 in order to observe the rockets' re-entrance into the atmosphere.*

which airflow was forced through shutters into a combustion chamber where a petrol fuel spray was ignited. The explosion closed the front shutters, forcing the expanding air out through a jet pipe at the rear. With the subsequent drop in pressure, the front shutters would open again, and the cycle repeated. This propelled the aircraft, carrying it's 850kg warhead, to a speed of 400mph to a maximum distance of 160 miles. But to create the necessary initial airflow through the engine the aircraft had to be shot into the air and then the pulse-jet would kick-in.

There were two ways in which this airflow could be generated. The first was to deploy it from a conventional bomber, the flying bomb achieving

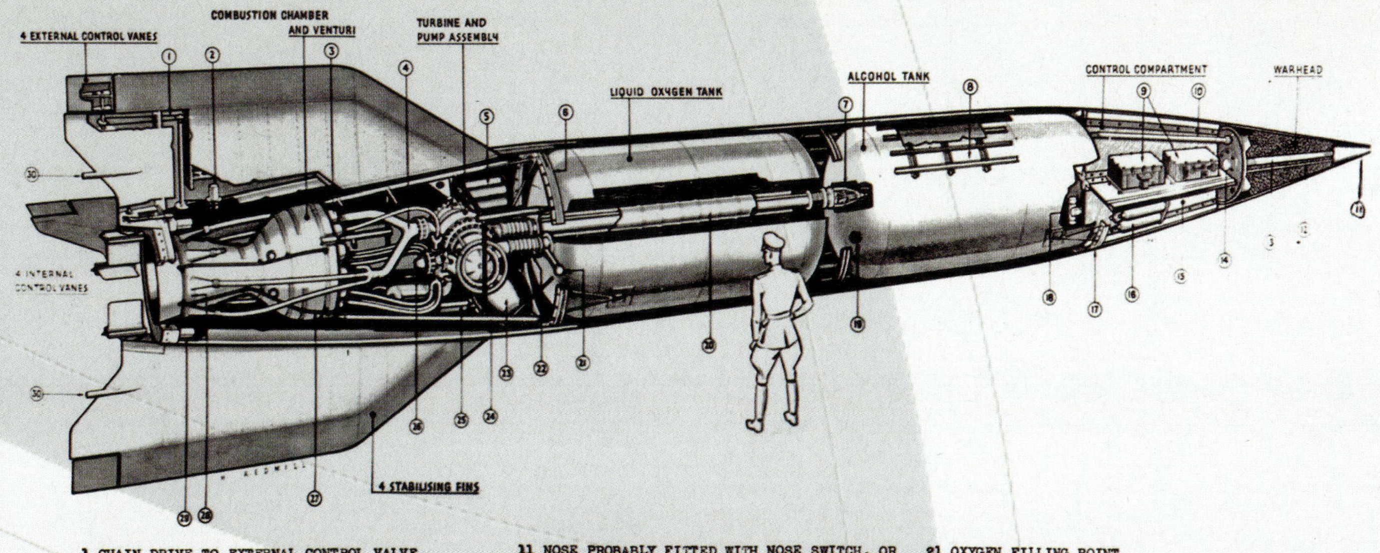

1 CHAIN DRIVE TO EXTERNAL CONTROL VALVE
2 ELECTRIC MOTOR
3 BURNER CUPS
4 ALCHOL SUPPLY FROM PUMP
5 AIR BOTTLES
6 REAR JOINT RING AND STRONG POINT FOR TRANSPORT
7 SERVO-OPERATED ALCOHOL OUTLET VALVE
8 ROCKET SHELL
9 RADIO EQUIPMENT
10 PIPE LEADING FROM ALCOHOL TANK TO WARHEAD
11 NOSE PROBABLY FITTED WITH NOSE SWITCH, OR OTHER DEVICE FOR OPERATING WARHEAD FUZE
12 CONDUIT CARRYING WIRES TO NOSE OF WARHEAD
13 CENTRAL EXPLODER TUBE
14 ELECTRIC FUZE FOR WARHEAD
15 PLYWOOD FRAME
16 NITROGEN BOTTLES
17 FRONT JOINT RING AND STRONG POINT FOR TRANSPORT
18 PITCH AND AZIMUTH GYROS
19 ALOCHOL FILLING POINT
20 DOUBLE WALLED ALCOHOL DELIVERY PIPE TO PUMP
21 OXYGEN FILLING POINT
22 CONCERTINA CONNECTIONS
23 HYDROGEN PEROXIDE TANK
24 TUBULAR FRAME HOLDING TURBINE AND PUMP ASSEMBLY
25 PERMANGANATE TANK (GAS GENERATOR UNIT BEHIND THIS TANK)
26 OXYGEN DISTRIBUTOR FROM PUMP
27 ALCOHOL PIPES FOR SUBSIDIARY COOLING
28 ALCOHOL INLET TO DOUBLE WALL
29 ELECTRO-HYDRAULIC SERVO MOTORS
30 AERIAL LEADS

the required airflow as it plummeted towards the ground. The other method, and the one that was initially adopted, was for the flying bomb to be propelled into the air from an inclined ramp by means of a powerful steam-driven catapult. The ramp would be pointed in the direction which the flying bomb was to travel, and distance to the target was determined by a mechanism which, at the appropriate moment, would force

the weapon into a steep power-dive. In reality, however, the dive caused the fuel flow to be interrupted, causing the engine to cut out.

Though undoubtedly a far less sophisticated machine than the A4, its very simplicity was its principal advantage over the rocket. This made it quicker, easier and cheaper to develop and manufacture than the A4. With both weapons appearing to work well in principle, all that was now required was to perfect them for deployment in the field before large-scale manufacture could commence.

'What I want is complete annihilation!'

The two programmes, though running in parallel, were also in direct competition with each other for resources and funding. The result of this was a 'shoot-off' between the two weapons on 26 May 1943, in front of a host of Reich dignitaries. Two of each type were fired. Both rockets sailed easily through the Baltic skies to a distance of 160 miles. Both flying bombs failed miserably. Though agreement was reached that there was room in the Wehrmacht armoury for both weapons, Dornberger's

> *"Why was it I could not believe in the success of your work? If we had had these rockets in 1939, we should never have had this war."*

programme was, at last, to receive all the support it needed.

Even Hitler was impressed when, on 7 July 1943, Dornberger was invited to the Wolfsschanze, the Führer's eastern headquarters, to deliver a presentation to him. At 17.00 hours, in the Wolfsschanze's cinema room, Hitler was shown a film of the A4, with von Braun providing the commentary. Hitler had never seen the rocket in the air and he sat there in silent fascination. When the film ended, Hitler walked over to von Braun and shook him by the hand. 'I thank you,' the Führer said, in almost a whisper. 'Why was it I could not believe in the success of your work? If we had had these rockets in 1939, we should never have had this war.'

The sight of the great, gleaming missiles soaring over the Baltic fired Hitler's imagination. He demanded 2,000 rockets a month to be fired at Britain: 'What I want is complete annihilation!'

Later that evening, back in his bunker with Speer, Hitler gushed enthusiastically about the A4, declaring that it was the weapon which would decide the war, and telling the munitions minister that Dornberger must be given all the ▶

labour and materials he needed. Hitler's sudden backing, however, came with much baggage.

Firstly, Himmler, always looking to his own position, tried to take the A4 programme under his own authority, insisting that the project was so important that it should be taken over by the SS of which he was the head. Hitler, wisely, demurred.

Secondly, Hitler set up a Development Commission for Long-Range Bombardment (Entwicklungs-commission für Fernschiessen) under Dr Waldemar Peterson to organise every aspect of the rocket and flying bomb organisations. According to those who then had to work under the auspices of this new bureaucratic body, it was an unnecessary 'clumsy, unwieldy conglomerate' which was soon to become embroiled in accusations of 'mismanagement and impropriety'.[2] All of this proved to be a drag on the rocket's development – indeed, at one point, on Thursday, 17 August 1943, Dornberger's senior staff threatened to resign en masse and return to academic life.

Peterson's commission was also supposed to decide which of the two weapons the effort should be concentrated on and, wisely, he suggested that both should be fully developed. That progression included the construction of huge concrete launch sites for the A4 in the Pas de Calais from where the rockets could be sent against Britain, and London in particular. Such vast structures were bound to attract the attention of the RAF and Dornberger preferred a number of highly mobile sites which Allied bombers would be unable to easily keep track of. Dornberger was overruled. But already, the RAF had begun to turn its attention to the strange activities at Peenemünde. ●

RIGHT *The moment that a German V-2 rocket is test-fired. The first test launch of a V2 occurred on 13 June 1942. The rocket pitched out of control and crashed as a result of a propellant feed system failure.* (HISTORIC MILITARY PRESS)

Eyes in the Sky

THOUGH SCRAPS OF INFORMATION ABOUT THE SECRET GERMAN ESTABLISHMENT AT PEENEMÜNDE REACHED LONDON, IT WAS THROUGH AERIAL PHOTOGRAPHY THAT THE TRUE NATURE OF THE SITE WAS FINALLY REVEALED.

It was in a café in Rouen in north-western France that a member of the independent *Réseau Agir* resistance group overheard two building contractors discussing the work they were engaged upon for the Germans. What struck the listener was that the workers were amazed at the extraordinary amount of concrete that was being used.

This intriguing snippet of information was passed onto the leader of the *Réseau Agir*, Michel Hollard, who went into Rouen the following day. Hollard did not know where this construction work was being carried out, though clearly it must have been somewhere local to Rouen. So, dressed in ecclesiastical-looking black attire, he went into the local official employment office armed with a collection of bibles. He announced that he was a representative of a Protestant organisation interested in the welfare of labouring men and he asked the officials if there were any building sites in the area. He was told that there was one at Auffay, about twenty miles from Rouen.

About an hour later, Hollard arrived at Auffay. He had changed into workman's clothes and he set about trying to find the building site. There were four roads leading

ABOVE *An example of one of the aircraft that did so much to reveal the secrets of the German V weapon programme pictured in flight in 1944. This is a de Havilland Mosquito PR Mk.XVI, that with the serial number NS502, of 544 Squadron, which was based at RAF Benson.* (VIA HISTORIC MILITARY PRESS)

from Auffay. On one of them he discovered a large clearing where several hundred men were at work. Sure enough, vast quantities of concrete were being poured and buildings were being erected. This demanded further investigation.

Hollard picked up a wheelbarrow from a ditch, loaded it with bricks and joined in the work. No-one challenged him. He questioned his new workmates when the opportunity arose but found that most of the labourers were foreign workers and few of them spoke French. Those that he could communicate with told him that they were building garages.

It was immediately obvious that this was not true. Firstly, the buildings were too small for garages and secondly, why would there be a need for so many garages so far from any town? What puzzled Hollard most of

he had better inform London.[1]

Michel Louis Hollard had been passing on information to Britain since the fall of France in 1940. A First World War veteran and holder of the *Croix de Guerre*, Hollard was an engineer at the Centre d'Etudes de Mécanique, Balistique et Armement and had been involved in the testing of prototypes for the armed forces. With the fall of France, Hollard was redundant but he quickly found employment with a company that produced gas engines which ran on charcoal rather than petrol which was in extremely short-supply throughout Europe.

In this guise – as the Paris representative of the Maison Gazogene Autobloc – Hollard had a legitimate reason to travel to the densely-wooded region that bordered Switzerland. What better place to look for charcoal?

After a series of astonishing adventures, Hollard managed to bluff

all was the fifty-yard strip of concrete with a guideline of blue string. When Hollard discreetly pulled out his pocket compass, he found that the concrete strip pointed directly at London!

As the other labourers clearly knew nothing, Hollard targeted the site foreman. Waiting until he saw the foreman heading for the toilets, Hollard followed him in and found him sat on one of the open row of seats. Hollard duly dropped his trousers and sat down beside the foreman. Taking out a packet of cigarettes, he offered one to the foreman and struck up a conversation. Hollard learnt from his new friend that the Germans were working the labourers in three eight-hour shifts non-stop around the clock, and that there were many other such sites under construction. Hollard decided that

his way into Switzerland across the heavily guarded Zone Rouge. Though he had risked his life to make contact with the British Embassy in Berne (he had in fact been travelling for four days and nights, mostly on foot or bicycle and had been arrested and spent two nights in custody), when he presented himself to the Assistant Military Attaché he received a cool reception. Incredibly, Hollard's offer to spy on the Germans and pass on intelligence was met with rejection. 'Switzerland was a neutral country', he was told, 'and it would be quite improper for the British Embassy ▶

to engage in espionage against a power with whom the Swiss were in friendly relation'.

Hollard returned to Paris disappointed but unbowed. He promised to return to Switzerland a month later, and he kept his word. This time, upon his arrival at the British Embassy, he received a far-different reception. The Military Attaché had checked Hollard's credentials and the Frenchman was asked if he could provide information in the Occupied Zone about German military formations, particularly armoured divisions. Hollard was now a recognised British spy.

Gradually, Hollard gathered around him like-minded people until his spy ring – the *Réseau Agir* – numbered no

less than sixty agents and the information his group had amassed and passed onto London had been found to be very accurate. Indeed only a few months earlier the *Réseau Agir* had identified the construction of a new naval dock at Marseilles (being built under the cover of an enormous shed) which had been disbelieved by British Intelligence. It was only when Hollard himself sneaked into the construction site and took photos with a Brownie box camera hidden under his jacket that the information was taken seriously. A few days later the RAF bombed the site into oblivion.

However, when he reported back to Switzerland with his news about the building work that was being carried out at high speed by the Germans, his contact was not overly impressed. Reports of strange buildings and curious constructions were far from uncommon and it usually transpired that they were something entirely innocuous. Yet Hollard was normally reliable and level-headed and, after the Marseille incident, no report of his

> *"When André put all the plans together in a detailed sketch it was quite apparent what the site was – it was a launching pad for some kind of missile aimed at London."*

could be dismissed. So, the information was passed onto London.

Hollard and his team, meanwhile, had toured the area around the Channel coast and by October had located an astonishing 100 possible sites. But Michel still did not know what the sites were. This problem troubled him almost constantly. One way or another, he had to find out what the Germans were planning.

As luck would have it, one of Hollard's group, who was employed by the Germans as an architectural draughtsman, was tasked to draw up plans for the next stage of site constructions. He was able to pass onto Hollard copies of all of the plans that he had drawn up. But this person – André Comps – was not permitted to know what was to be erected on top of the numerous concrete strips. That information was held on a large blue-print by the German officer in charge at the site where André was based. The officer kept the blue-print in his coat pocket and it never left his side

– except when he went to the latrine. Once again, a key part of this drama would be played out in a French toilet.

André noticed that the officer went to the latrine block every morning for three to five minutes. So, one day André waited until the officer was sitting comfortably on the toilet reading the morning paper before stealing the blue-print and copying down the secret details.

When André put all the plans together in a detailed sketch it was quite apparent what the site was – it was a launching pad for some kind of missile aimed at London. There could no longer be any doubt, the Germans were preparing to mount a massive attack at the very heart of the UK.

The special flight

When reports of Hollard's findings reached London, they came as no surprise to some Air Ministry officials. On 19 September 1939, after the invasion of Poland, Hitler told the world in a speech from Danzig that Germany had a secret weapon and MI.6, Britain's secret service, had been tasked to investigate. The man appointed to conduct the investigation was a twenty-seven-year-old physicist, Dr Reginald Victor Jones, often referred to as R.V. Jones, who was transferred from his work at the Royal Aircraft Factory at Farnborough.

As Jones set about his job, an astonishing package landed on his desk in November of that same year. The package had been sent by Captain Hector Boyes, the British Naval Attaché in the Norwegian capital, Oslo. It contained a seven-page typed

TOP *One of the surviving buildings at Bois Carré. It can clearly be seen on the reconnaissance photographs as the large, elongated structure almost directly in the middle of the wood. It is the main assembly workshop, which is divided into three sections – one for fitting out, a second for repairs and the third for spare parts.* (HISTORIC MILITARY PRESS)

ABOVE LEFT *Inside the fitting out section of the main assembly workshop at Bois Carré.* (HISTORIC MILITARY PRESS)

ABOVE MIDDLE *The walls of the launch ramp at Bois Carré.* (JOHN GREHAN)

report and a glass fuse. The report detailed, among other technical advances supposedly achieved by German scientists, information concerning the development of rocket technology at a place called Peenemünde and of new types of fuses – as demonstrated in the example sent in the package. Many years after the war, in his last will and testament, the German scientist, Hans Ferdinand Mayer, revealed that he had been the man who leaked what has become known as the 'Oslo Report'.

Confirmation of these activities was urgently required. With access to the site strictly controlled, only two methods of acquiring the necessary information were available – that of intercepted signals intelligence and aerial observation. It would be a combination of both of these that would unlock the secrets of Peenemünde.

Even before the receipt of the Oslo Report, the importance of obtaining intelligence from aerial observation of the enemy had prompted the creation, on 22 September 1939, of a top-secret 'Special Flight' under the auspices of Fighter Command, to conduct aerial photography over enemy territory. The aircraft this Special Flight would operate – under the guise of No.2

Camouflage Unit – was to be the Supermarine Spitfire, the fastest British aircraft of the day, stripped of all non-essential equipment, including its guns, ammunition and radio, being reliant upon speed and altitude to stay out of danger. Later de Haviland Mosquitoes were also used.

The initial photographs obtained by

ABOVE *A vital weapon in the battle against the V weapons, an aerial camera, in this case a Type F.8 Mk.II, is loaded into the vertical position in a Spitfire PR Mk.IV at RAF Benson.* (VIA HISTORIC MILITARY PRESS)

LEFT *Thanks in great part to Michel Hollard's reports and information from his agents, the V1 launch sites in France were systematically bombed by the Royal Air Force from mid-December 1943 and for much of 1944. Evidence of this bombardment can be seen in this shot of the main assembly workshop at Bois Carré. The editor is pictured standing in a large bomb crater – which can be seen just next to the bottom of the building in the post attack reconnaissance photograph on page 15.* (HISTORIC MILITARY PRESS)

the Special Flight were disappointing. They had been taken from such a high altitude that they were of little value. The small team of just six Photograph Interpreters was unable to garner much useful information from the 1/80,000-scale images. That was until the photographs were sent to a civilian company which had been lobbying for work, Aerofilms Limited. The company seized the opportunity it had been given and there Michael Spender was able to produce a three-dimensional analysis of the photographs using a machine the company had purchased the previous year from Switzerland, which was known as the Wild Machine.

So effective were the analyses that the company was incorporated into the Air Ministry, more Photograph Interpreters were recruited, and the operating body of the aircraft became the Photographic Reconnaissance Unit or PRU.[2] With information supplied from Bletchley Park, where intercepted German communications were decrypted to provide context to what was seen through the camera lens, and the detail provided by the Wild Machine, all the pieces were gradually put in place to conduct accurate photographic reconnaissance and to find out what was really going on at Peenemünde.

Long-range projectors

The greatly increased interpretation team – soon to be part of a much larger Central Interpretation Unit – was transferred from the dangers of London to Medmenham, a picturesque village in Buckinghamshire, where ▶

it took over the neo-Tudor pile of Danesfield House. The other elements of the CIU included a team of model-makers at RAE Farnborough who used photographs taken by the PRU aircraft to build models of particular targets on request. The PRU itself moved to RAF Benson in Oxfordshire on Boxing Day 1940. The photographic reconnaissance operation continued to expand, providing information for all three services of the armed forces. Such were the demands for its services, it was not until 1943 that the attention of the CIU was focused on the activities at Peenemünde.

This was prompted by a memorandum from MI.14, a branch of the Directorate of Military Intelligence that specialized in obtaining intelligence about Germany. The memorandum stated that there had recently been indications that the Germans might be developing 'some form of long-range projectors' capable of firing a projectile which could reach Britain from the French coast. The only information available to the War Office was that the projector might be similar in form to a section of railway track. The CIU was asked to look out for 'suspicious erections of rails or scaffolding'.

The following month, on 22 March 1943, further indications of the development of some kind of

secret weapon came from a recorded discussion between two high-ranking German generals who had been captured at the Second Battle of El Alamein. The two had been kept apart until they could be secretly recorded in the hope that when they met, they would reveal useful information. In their discussion at Trent Park, General der Panzertruppe Wilhelm Ritter von Thoma told General der Panzertruppe Ludwig Crüwell about what he had once seen on a visit to Kummersdorf: 'I saw it once with Feldmarschall Brauchitsch. There is a special ground near Kunersdorf [*sic*] they've got these huge things which they've brought

up here ... They've always said they would go 15 km into the stratosphere and then ... You only aim at an area ... If one was to ... every few days ... frightful ... The major there was full of hope. He said, "Wait until next year and the fun will start!".'

Clearly every effort had to be made to discover exactly what these 'huge things' were and where they were being built. This was put to Winston Churchill by General Hastings Ismay, Chief of Staff to the Minister of Defence, in a minute dated 15 April 1943: 'Prime Minister, The Chiefs of Staff feel that you should be made aware of reports of German

experiments with long-range rockets. The fact that five reports have been received since the end of 1942 indicates a foundation of fact even if details are inaccurate. The Chiefs of Staff are of an opinion that no time should be lost in establishing the facts, and, if the evidence proves reliable, in devising countermeasures. They feel this is a case where investigation by one man who could call on such scientific and intelligence advisers as might be appropriate would give the best and quickest results.'[3]

The man the Chiefs of Staff recommended was Duncan Sandys, the thirty-five-year-old Joint

> *"Prime Minister, The Chiefs of Staff feel that you should be made aware of reports of German experiments with long-range rockets."*

Parliamentary Secretary to the Ministry of Supply and Member of Parliament for South Norwood. In his position with the Ministry of Supply, Sandys was responsible for all weapons research, development and production. As a lieutenant colonel, Sandys had also led the first British 'Rocket Regiment' based at the Projectile Development Establishment in Wales. He was uniquely placed to draw together all the people he needed to uncover the German secret weapons programme. He was appointed to his new role just five days after Churchill had received Ismay's note.

German long-range rocket detection

The teams at RAF Medmenham were told that the new weapon, which was now firmly understood to be a rocket, had a range of 130 miles and that they should look for the weapon in the Peenemünde area where it was believed tests were being conducted, as well as places in France within 130 miles of London. All photographs taken of this vast area since 1 January 1943, were to be re-examined and gaps in the coverage were to be filled by the PRU. The interpreters were told to look out for a long range-gun or tube, possibly in an unused mine from where the rocket could be fired.

Though unaware at the time, a photograph of rockets at Peenemünde had been taken by a PRU plane on 15 May 1942. On flight A/762, Flight Lieutenant Donald Steventon was tasked with photographing the port of Swinemunde and had switched on his camera while passing over the airfield at Peenemünde. Since that date, Peenemünde had been photographed three further times, in January, March and April 1943. These photographs were studied very carefully, but it was concluded that what would later be identified as launching ramps for the V1 were pumping machines related to land reclamation. The first report on activities at Peenemünde stated that the site was not yet in full use and that there was no evidence of any rockets having got beyond the experimental stage, and that there was no immediate threat to the UK. Nevertheless, there was sufficient activity at Peenemünde to warrant frequent monitoring. This was formalized under the title of German

Long-Range Rocket Detection.

This frequent monitoring – twice a week – soon produced some very interesting photographs. This included one taken on 2 June in which a 'thick vertical column about 40ft high and 4 feet thick' was seen. When the photograph was shown to R.V. Jones, he firmly believed that he could see the outline of a rocket. This was confirmed without question when photographs taken by the PRU's Flight Sergeant Ernest Peek, who was at the controls of a de Havilland Mosquito PR Mark IX of 540 Squadron, showed quite distinctly a large rocket.[4]

Reports from forced labourers at Peenemünde had also been received from the Continent. This included letters smuggled out of Peenemünde by a Luxembourger, Henri Roth, to his father who was a member of a Belgian resistance cell, in which he described the rocket testing. In putting all the evidence together, including

information from Bletchley Park, one of the team leaders at Medmenham, Wing Commander Hugh Hamshaw Thomas, arranged for the model makers to create a scale model of the Peenemünde site based solely on the known facts.

Bodyline

The model and the photographs were discussed at the first meeting of the Bodyline Scientific Co-Ordinating Committee on 26 July 1943. Chaired by Sandys, this group of scientists, which included R.V. Jones, was asked to put forward an explanation of how the Peenemünde site functioned and to determine what was happening there. The members were told to make an appointment to see the models and photographs which were held under lock and key by the Ministry of Economic Warfare, and then compile their report. *Bodyline* ▶

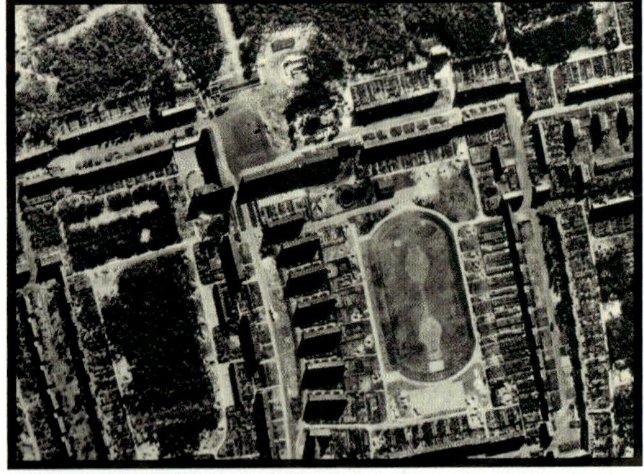

became the codename for operations against all phases of the German long-range weapons programme.

Though there still remained no immediate threat from the weapons being tested at Peenemünde, it was clear that considerable effort was being put into the operations at the site and that it would be unwise to allow the Germans to continue their work there unimpeded. Air Marshal Sir Arthur Harris, the Commander-in-Chief of the RAF's Bomber Command, was therefore approached on 7 July to add Peenemünde to his list of targets.

The Baltic, though, was a long way from the UK and, being mid-summer, the nights were short, which meant that no missions against Peenemünde by Harris' heavy bombers could take place immediately. Harris was also at pains to point out that his crews were unable to hit specific objects and only able to conduct 'area' bombing. Accuracy would be further reduced by the giant smoke machines known to be present at Peenemünde and which could blanket the site with dense smokescreen.

While Bomber Command waited for the longer nights, the Target Section at RAF Medmenham produced a detailed site plan of Peenemünde for Harris' crews, along with annotated aerial photographs explaining the nature of the buildings, and the location of anti-aircraft guns and searchlights. All that the crews were told of Peenemünde was that it was an experimental

TOP *A Mosquito PR Mk.XVI of 544 Squadron – this aircraft, NS502, is that which appears on page 14.* (CLAVEWORK GRAPHICS)

ABOVE *Also taken by Flight Sergeant Peek, this photograph shows one of the key target areas for Bomber Command in the early hours of 18 August 1943 – the sleeping and living quarters at Peenemünde.* (HISTORIC MILITARY PRESS)

RIGHT *The Luftwaffe Test Installation at Peenemünde West. The original caption states that, 'ramps (A) were used for launching the flying bombs over the Baltic Sea', whilst 'two prototype flying bombs can be seen at (B)'.* (HISTORIC MILITARY PRESS)

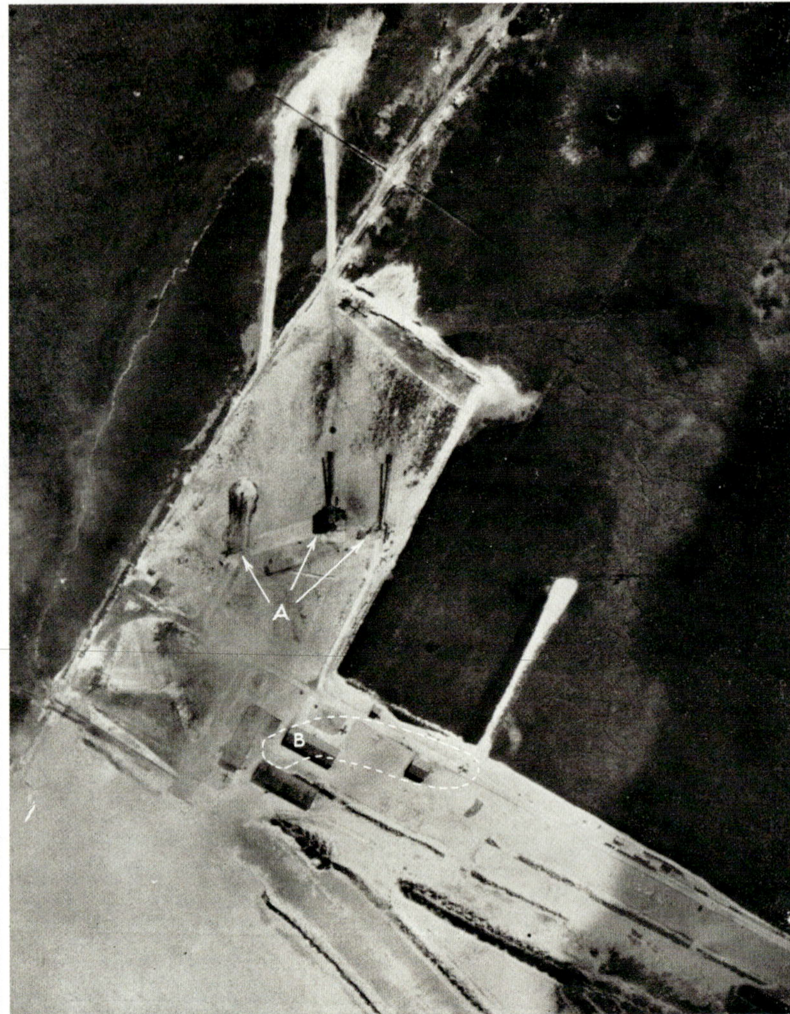

site, chiefly of importance in the manufacture of high-concentration hydrogen peroxide. Seven targets were identified: Experimental Station, Factory Workshops, Power Plant, Unidentified Apparatus, Experimental Establishment, Sleeping and Living Quarters and the Experimental Airfield. Though the true nature of the site was not disclosed to the airmen, its extreme importance was clear when they were told that if their first mission failed to destroy the Peenemünde installations, it would be repeated every night 'regardless, within practicable limits, of casualties'.

The night of 17/18 August was chosen for the raid on Peenemünde. It was code-named Operation *Hydra*. ●

Operation Hydra

THERE WAS NO LONGER ANY DOUBT THAT THE GERMANS WERE DEVELOPING A BALLISTIC MISSILE AT PEENEMÜNDE, AND BOMBER COMMAND WAS GIVEN THE TASK OF DESTROYING THE SITE'S FACILITIES.

Almost 600 heavy bombers, Lancasters, Halifaxes, and Stirlings, along with Mosquitoes, were detailed for the attack upon Peenemünde. These aircraft would be flying deep into enemy territory, and into the midst of the German night fighters. A diversion was therefore planned, in which aircraft from the Pathfinder Force – a group which located and marked targets with flares – would fly over Berlin and, hopefully, attract the attention of the German fighters. The Pathfinders were to set off seventy-five minutes before the main force and would take a northerly route past Peenemünde. When the main force appeared to be following a similar flight plan as the Pathfinders, it was hoped that the Luftwaffe would await its arrival closer to its bases near the capital of the Third Reich. By the time that the Germans realised the target was not Berlin, the bombers would be on their way home.

The housing estate where the scientist and technicians lived was to be the first aiming point. This was on the insistence of Sandys, Harris wanting to strike just at the two large workshop buildings. But in line with the policy of area bombing adopted in February 1942, in which Bomber Command was instructed to attack the German civilian population as well as its military assets, killing the key people at Peenemünde was a logical, if distasteful, step. The workshop buildings were second on the list, with the Development Works last. Zero Hour was to be 00.15 hours on 18 August.

The attack upon Peenemünde was to be delivered in three waves. Three other aircraft from the Pathfinder Force were assigned to Peenemünde – one for each of the three waves of the attacking main force which would drop coloured target indicator flares on the three aiming points in turn.

The whole attack was to last for forty-five minutes. The first wave of bombers would saturate the scientists' housing estate, and after four minutes, during which the Pathfinders would drop target-indicators on the second aiming point, a further swift attack would be launched on the two huge workshops. Finally, the Pathfinders would illuminate the

ABOVE *German anti-aircraft fire over Peenemünde, as photographed from one of the RAAF Lancasters involved in Operation Hydra.* (AUSTRALIAN WAR MEMORIAL; P02018.229)

third aiming point, the Peenemünde Development Works.

As they gathered for the pre-operational briefing, the crews knew that they were about to take part in something out of the ordinary. Flying Officer Bill Day was with 90 Squadron at RAF Tuddenham: 'This was the only briefing I ever went to when the briefing hut was surrounded by Service Police. We had to go to the door with the crew and show our identification with our pilot. We were told that if a word leaked out about the target we wouldn't go that night and the source would be summarily executed.'

Security was equally tight across all the participating airfields. Sergeant Charles Cawthorne was with 467

Squadron at RAF Bottesford: 'There was a great buzz of speculation amongst the crews as we entered the large briefing room … The curtain over the map of Western Europe was pulled back to reveal red route marker tapes leading to a small target called Peenemünde on the German Baltic coast sited between Rostock and Stettin. I wondered what all the fuss was about because we had never heard of this little place called Peenemünde.'[1]

The crews were told that they would be attacking the site where a new form of radiolocation equipment was being developed which would improve the effectiveness of the German night-fighter operations. In order to hamper the production of this equipment it was necessary to destroy both the Experimental Station and the large factory workshops, and to kill or incapacitate the scientific and technical personnel working there.

Eight Mosquitoes from 139 Squadron were to undertake the diversionary attack on Berlin, each dropping marker flares and a minimal bombload, after switching on their radio equipment to lay a false scent across Germany. They would also be deploying a cloud of small, thin strips of black paper backed with aluminium foil which was referred to by the codename *Window*. These strips reflected radar signals and gave a mass of false readings on radar screens making it impossible for the radar operators to determine the true scale of the attack.

German preparöness

The approach over the North Sea was to be made at very low level; the bombers would creep in under the German radar. Reaching Denmark, the whole armada would climb fast to 7,000 feet, from which altitude most aircraft would attack their targets. At 21.00 hours on the 17th, the first bombers were taxiing into the wind.

A brilliant moon was rising in a cloudless sky.

The Germans, though, were far from unaware that Bomber Command were preparing for a major operation, as their radio monitoring service reported that the air was thick with test transmissions from British bombers. As it happened, that night, for the first time, single-seater aircraft from the day-fighter force would operate alongside the twin-engine night-fighters. The Luftwaffe had no inkling of the target or targets of the British bombers, but they were able to determine that the raid would be against northern Germany and not anywhere in southern Germany, as communications had been intercepted warning the coastal defences at Cromer in Norfolk of the fact that aircraft would be flying out and back across the North Sea at that point.

With German stations on alert, it was the Danish coastguard units which first detected the Pathfinders and this information was passed to Oberstleutnant Hajo Herrmann, the creator and commander of the Luftwaffe's recently formed night fighter wing, Jagdgeschwader 300, at Bonn-Hangelar airfield. Hermann immediately telephoned Generaloberst Hubert Weise in Berlin. In their discussion they concluded that the likely target was the German capital.

The Pathfinders crossed the Danish coast a little after 22.00 hours, deploying copious quantities of *Window* as they crossed the west coast of Usedom island and then turned south towards the German capital. Herrmann's night fighters were scrambled, with more than 200 fighters taking to the air in what was the largest effort of its kind so far in the war. But the Mosquitos were ▶

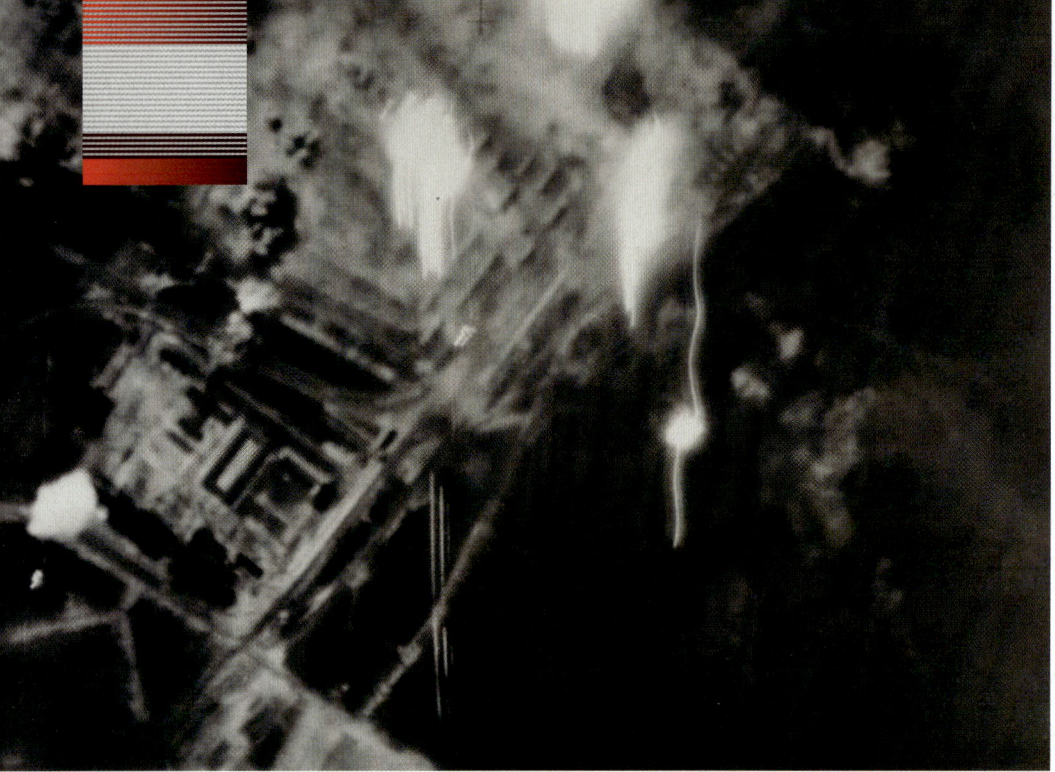

return to their homes on the housing estate. For some it would prove to be a fatal decision.

The first indication that Peenemünde was going to be attacked was when the flares began to drop from the Pathfinders with the main bomber force. These were not all dropped with great accuracy due to patches of cloud in the bright moonlight, many of the flares landing two miles southeast of the housing estate, and when the second wave attacked a light wind had blown some of the markers into the sea. The Master Bomber for the operation was Group Captain John H. Searby, the CO of 83 Squadron. This raid marked the first occasion that Bomber Command used a Master Bomber to control the attack of the Main Force. 'Suddenly, the area was lit up by brilliant light from the flares,' recalled Searby, 'as the first wave of Pathfinders passed over and red target indicators dropped in dazzling cascade to the ground'.

ABOVE *Bombs can be seen bursting among the buildings at Peenemünde in the early hours of 18 August 1943.* (AUSTRALIAN WAR MEMORIAL; SUK11314)

RIGHT *A Halifax II of 51 Squadron, HR952 coded MH-X, at Snaith in the summer of 1943 – at about the time of the unit's participation in Operation Hydra.* (COURTESY OF ANDREW THOMAS)

much quicker than the more stately heavy bombers and 139 Squadron's planes were over Berlin at 22.56 hours with the German fighters far in their wake amidst a swirling mass of tiny aluminium strips. By this time the main bomber stream had been detected over the North Sea and it appeared that Berlin was about to suffer a major attack.

The previous month, July 1943, Hamburg had been attacked by Bomber Command and the USAAF Eighth Air Force for eight days and nights without cessation, causing a massive firestorm which swept through the German city. Most of Hamburg was destroyed and more than 40,000 of its citizens killed. The raid that was now unfolding could well be the start of a similar operation against Berlin. As the sirens wailed their warnings throughout the city, the call went out for every night fighter to come to the defence of the capital of the Third Reich.

The air raid sirens had also sounded at Peenemünde where von Braun's private secretary, Dorette Kersten, had been enjoying a walk in the bright moonlight: 'First of all I go to my room; there's no hurry, this is not the first time it's only been a warning. My room-mate is still there, wildly packing her bags; I laugh in her face,

only pick up a book and drape a bathing-wrap round my shoulders in case it gets too cold.

'We make our way out. By Block Thirty a number of men from the West Works [of the Luftwaffe] are standing around, looking up at the clear sky and cracking jokes; they laugh at her suitcases! The bunker in front of Block Four is almost empty, a few people are clustered outside it. Most of them are going back to bed, as nothing seems to be happening.'

This delay, between the passing of the Pathfinders of 139 Squadron and the arrival of the main bomber force, did indeed encourage many to leave the safety of the air raid shelters and

Satisfied that enough of the markers had landed in the correct area, Searby ordered the first wave of the Main Force to commence its bombing run. The time was 00.17, two minutes later than planned.

The bombing was to be at an unusually low height, at 4,000 feet, with the objective of improving accuracy. But the crews knew that would make them more susceptible to anti-aircraft fire and if their aircraft were hit at such an altitude there was little chance of being able to parachute to safety in time before the bomber hit the ground. All they could do, though, was press on.

'That run-in was perilous in the extreme,' recalled Sergeant Ron James in a 90 Squadron Stirling. 'There was a mass of machines concentrated above over a very small target and despite the bombs whistling down … the explosions from the ground tossed us around like a cork. Meanwhile, the Germans had found a few score guns to supplement those twelve we had been led to expect. They didn't have to aim; just hosepipe straight up.'

Group Captain Searby watched the devastating impact of the bombs: 'By now the target was beginning to assume the familiar spectacle of a target under massive attack; bursting bombs, masses of billowing smoke through which the sliding beams of the searchlights crossed and re-crossed. The red bursts from heavy anti-aircraft mingled with it all … the target area was rapidly becoming a veritable inferno in which it became increasingly difficult to identify the various features.'[2]

A sea of flames

It was in her diary that Dorette Kersten wrote of the events of that night: 'Block Four is burning fiercely, and Block Five is in flames. Things are still exploding everywhere – time bombs. Rafters are falling in, gables collapsing.

'I nearly ran into a large pool of blood; there is a torn-off, uniformed leg lying in it. "Everybody out of the bunker and come and help!" What a disgrace, some people are slinking away. My Professor [Braun] shouts: "We must rescue the secret documents!" But the roof has already collapsed, and the gable will fall in any moment, too. We can still try the staircase.

'The Professor grips my hand and we move carefully in. The building is a mass of crackling flames. Groping along the wall, we reach the second floor. The doors have burnt away, but pressing tightly to the wall, because the other half of the floor has been swept away, we edge up to the safe.

'I run up and down the stairs several times, laden with secret papers, until I can keep going no longer. The Professor and some men stay up there throwing all the furniture and things out of the window. I stand by down

below, throwing the papers into a safe lying in the open on its back.

'The heat is tremendous. A sentry comes and stands stolidly in front of the safe, rifle at the ready. Slowly the dawn breaks. I return to the air-raid shelter. The secret papers are safely under lock and key.'[3]

Other witnesses described, 'a tremendous cloud of smoke, clearly visible in the night sky, lit by the glow of fire – a veritable sea of flames'. Another saw 'great fountains caused by the bombs which landed in the water'. From a distance the sight of the burning buildings was, 'almost spectral – a ghostly apparition'.[4]

Similar sights were seen from above. Sergeant W.L. Millar in a Lancaster of 460 Squadron, which formed part of the second wave, saw 'just a jumble of fire and wreckage'. Similarly, Sergeant Farmer's 101 Squadron was also in the second wave: 'The target looked as though one wave of bombers had already hit it and that the whole country was erupting into something terrible. The explosions below were so tremendous that, as we made our pass over the area, it was like riding a car over a ploughed field'.[5]

Oberleutnant Werner Magirius was Dornberger's adjutant: 'I only woke when I heard the noise of guns and of bombs in the distance. I opened the windows and saw smoke everywhere. I actually saw aircraft against the

ABOVE LEFT *Flight Sergeant Daniel Rees is pictured in the cockpit of his 460 Squadron RAAF Lancaster, showing the damage caused by a night fighter attack during Operation Hydra.* (AUSTRALIAN WAR MEMORIAL; UK0387)

ABOVE RIGHT *Two of Flight Sergeant Daniel Rees' crew, Flight Sergeant J. Venning (on the left) and Sergeant C.W. Harris, show the damage to their Lancaster, Mk.III ED985.* (AUSTRALIAN WAR MEMORIAL; UK0393)

BELOW *Another of the RAF squadrons that were involved in Hydra was 218 (Gold Coast) Squadron. It is one of its Stirling IIIs, that coded HA-S, which is pictured here at RAF Downham Market in 1943.* (COURTESY OF ANDREW THOMAS)

moonlight, and it was only then that I realised we were being attacked … I dressed quickly but not in panic … I was determined to be dressed correctly … I set off for the shelter, a little distance away … I found General Dornberger had reached it ahead of me …

'Then the bombing seemed to be all around us; we could feel the shock waves through the ground of the nearby hits before we heard their explosion … It eventually diminished and stopped altogether … We opened the door and found that there were no more aeroplane engines to be heard. We went out of the shelter and saw many of the surrounding buildings were on fire. I shall always remember exactly what General Dornberger said: "Mein schönes Peenemünde!" – "My beautiful Peenemünde!"; he said with great sadness. I think he meant not just Peenemünde but all the fine work that had been done there and with which he had been associated – the spirit of Peenemünde'.[6]

Bewilderment over Berlin

Some 120 miles to the south, 158 German night fighters were swarming over Berlin along with fifty-five day fighters. The sky above the German capital was a scene of utter confusion with the Luftwaffe pilots shooting at each other and the anti-aircraft gunners, bewildered and panicked at seeing so ▶

many aircraft, were firing at everything – 11,774 rounds of heavy anti-aircraft shells were fired that night.

Slowly, though, the evident non-sighting of British heavy bombers was causing one or two senior figures to wonder if the whole thing had been a giant hoax. Herrmann himself was flying a Focke-Wulf Fw 190 over Berlin when he saw Pathfinder flares dropping to the north over Peenemünde. At that point he realised that he and his colleagues had been deceived. Like the rest of the defenders, Herrmann was by this time low on fuel. Before he could fly to Peenemünde he had to land and refuel, as did many of his pilots. Some, though, were able to make their way directly to the Baltic.

The first two bomber waves delivered their payloads upon Peenemünde uninterrupted by anything other than ground fire. It would be a different matter for the third wave of 117 Lancasters of 5 Group and fifty-two Halifax and nine Lancaster bombers of 6 Group. Five German fighters caught the bombers in the act, shooting down twelve in as many minutes, with Group Captain Searle seeing 'showering fragments of exploding aircraft'. Twenty-nine of that final attack were shot down.

The destruction of one of these bombers was described by Unteroffizier Walter Hölker of Nachtjagdgeschwader 5, whose Messerschmitt Bf 110 was one of two specially adapted with twin cannon pointing upwards through the cockpit to enable the aircraft to fly underneath an enemy bomber and fire into its exposed belly: 'We were over 8,500 metres high by the time I reached the target area ... I saw, much lower, a whole lot of bombers flying east to west against the fire and smoke over the target. They looked like ants, crawling over the ground. I dived, but too quickly, far too fast to aim and shoot, and flew right past the bombers. I had to circle back again.

'Then Werner Zahi, my radar man, said he could see a Halifax ahead and above. I reduced speed and let it come over us ... I flew right up under him, so close that I couldn't see the sky, only this huge aeroplane. Then I pressed the button aiming as best I

MIDDLE LEFT *Another target photograph taken during the attack on 18 August 1943. The beach is that on the east side of Peenemünde, and the buildings that the bombs are falling on may well be those in the area of the hydrogen peroxide plant.* (AUSTRALIAN WAR MEMORIAL; SUK11313)

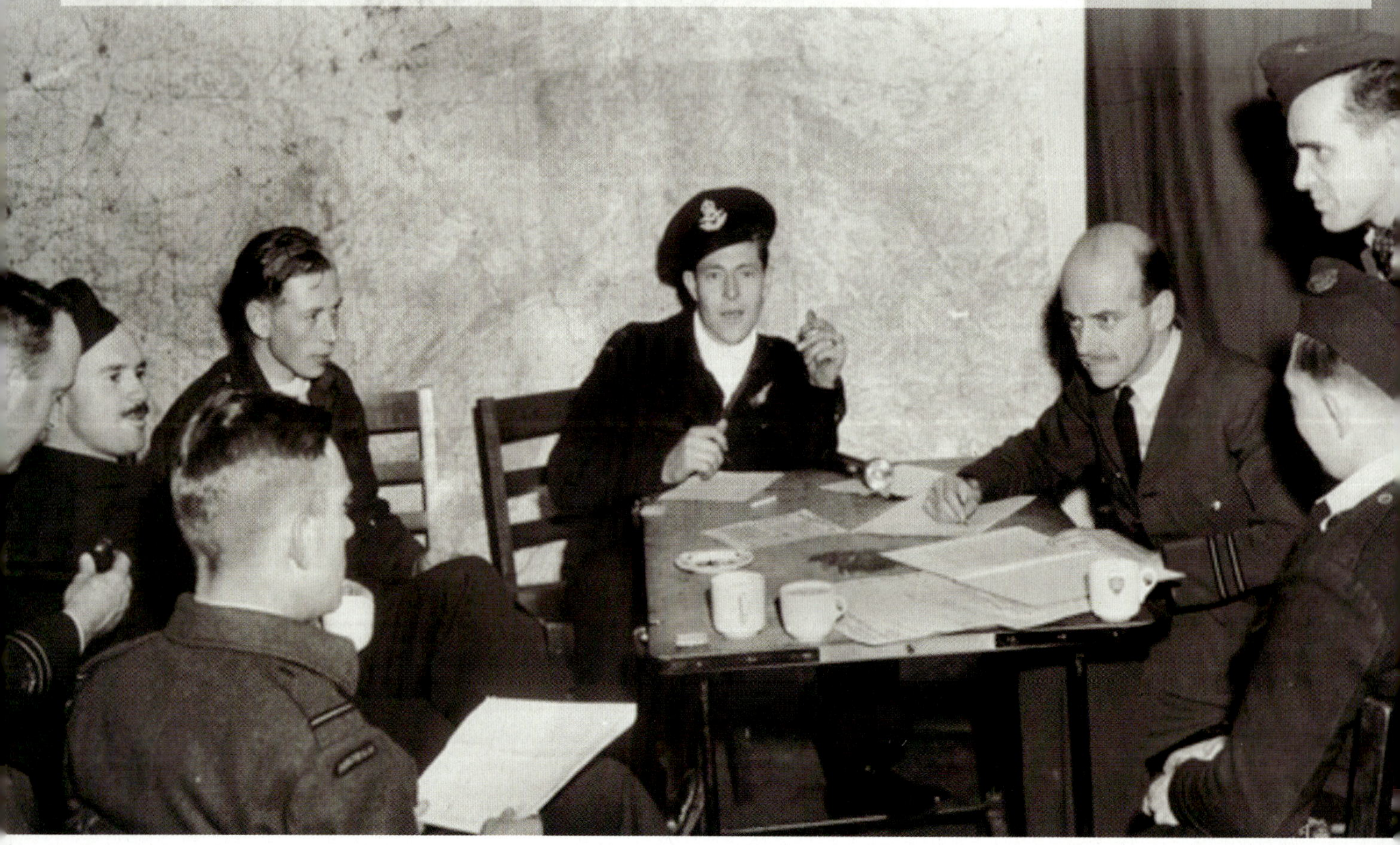

BELOW *In the immediate aftermath of the raid, aircrew from 460 Squadron RAAF are pictured being debriefed at RAF Binbrook.* (AUSTRALIAN WAR MEMORIAL; UK0401)

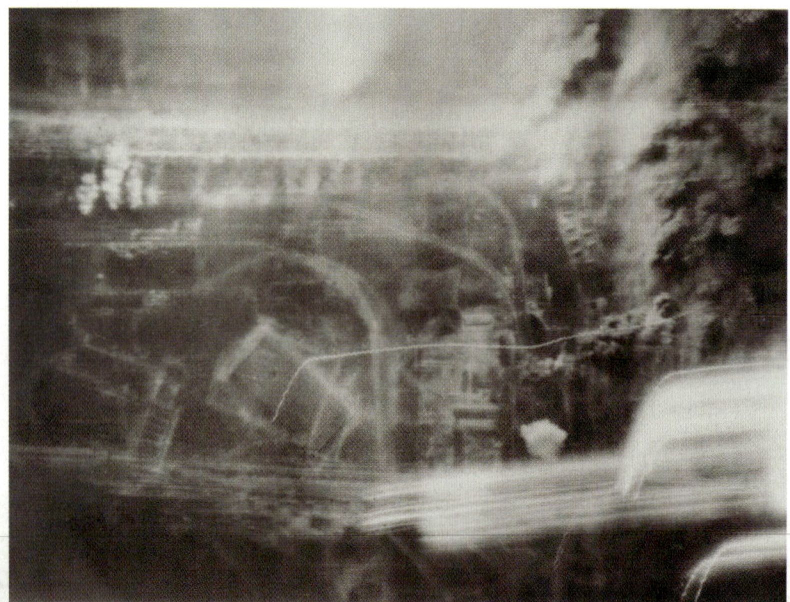

could at the inner left engine. I only fired four or six shots and the petrol immediately came pouring out on fire and the bomber started to go down.'[7]

As the bombers retreated across Denmark and the North Sea, others were caught by the German fighters. Altogether, forty-one aircraft were lost; twenty-three Lancasters, fifteen Halifaxes, two Stirlings and one Mosquito over Berlin. Only thirty German pilots claimed to have reached Peenemünde. Twelve of the Luftwaffe fighters were shot down or crashed.

was able to state: 'There is a large concentration of craters in and around the target area, and many buildings are still on fire. In the North Manufacturing Area [the Development Works] some twenty-seven buildings of medium size have been completely destroyed; at least four buildings are seen still burning.'

The bombing was exceptionally accurate, as revealed by the analysis of 457 bombing photographs. Bomber Command's Operational Research Section found that, 'it is

'Long live the Führer!'

A PRU Mosquito overflew Peenemünde soon after 10.00 hours on the morning after the raid. The photographs taken by the Mosquito were immediately passed onto Medmenham, and the CIU Interpretation Report

> *"In the North Manufacturing Area [the Development Works] some twenty-seven buildings of medium size have been completely destroyed..."*

probable that nearly all aircraft bombed within three miles, and the majority within one mile of the aiming point.' More detailed analysis revealed that in the Development Works fifty buildings had been seriously damaged; referring to Block Four, housing von Braun's administrative and drawing offices, it

found that, 'a long building, of which the greater part is useless, is now seen to be divided up into numerous small and large rooms, which suggests laboratory accommodation'.

The housing estate had suffered the worst damage, with every one of the 100 buildings having been demolished. The Trassenheide forced labour camp had also been severely damaged with eighteen of its thirty packed huts demolished. The water pumping station was also hit, meaning that there was no running water to any part of the site.

There were three notable casualties of the raid. Dr Walter Thiel, the chief engineer of rocket motors, and Dr Erich Walther, chief engineer of the rocket factory, were killed in one of the air-raid trenches, and the Chief of Air Staff, Generaloberst ▶

Among the latter were several Luxembourg labourers, including Henri Roth who had provided such useful information to Britain's secret services. Two hundred and forty-five Bomber Command crew were killed and forty-five taken prisoner.

Hans Jeschonnek, also died. When he learned of how his defensive forces had been completely deceived by a handful of Mosquitoes, he was found by his secretary lying on the floor, dead, a revolver in his hand. Next to the body was a note: 'I cannot work with Goering any more. Long live the Führer!' This was, seemingly, because Reichsmarschall Hermann Goering, Supreme Commander of the Luftwaffe, had blamed Jeschonnek for the lack of coordination between the anti-aircraft guns and the fighters over Berlin.

Total deaths at Peenemünde amounted to 732, of whom 120 were German staff, while the rest consisted of Russians, Poles, and other nationalities.

> *"There is no question that Operation* Hydra *put back the development of the A4 by many weeks. Just how serious a setback the bombing was remains uncertain."*

A4 by many weeks. Just how serious a setback the bombing was remains uncertain. The loss of Walther Thiel in particular was a severe blow, but how much this affected the programme cannot be accurately judged. What can be accurately

Vengeance weapons

There is no question that Operation *Hydra* put back the development of the

measured is the time between the last rocket test before the raid and the first one after. Before the raid, the team at Peenemünde had been testing one rocket on average every twelve days. The first rocket launched after *Hydra*, was test fired on 6 October – forty-eight days later. This was thirty-six days longer than was the case before the raid.

Therefore, though many different figures have been put forward, statistically, five to six weeks were initially lost on the rocket programme. This may not seem a particularly long time, but that was only part of the story. It had been made abundantly clear that Peenemünde was no longer a secret

site and that it was vulnerable to attack anytime that the Allies chose. In particular, it had been the policy of targeting civilians which paid the richest dividends. With the housing estate completely wrecked, immediate steps were put in hand following *Hydra* to evacuate the scientific personnel and the foreign labourers. The estate was abandoned and never rebuilt.

So it was, that four days after the raid, Hitler and Speer decided to move most of the A4 testing to Poland which was beyond the practical reach of the inquisitive PRU aircraft and the range of the heavy Allied bombers, and where there was abundant slave labour in the many concentration camps. In Poland it would also be possible to conduct tests against land targets and with live explosives – something that Braun was eager to attempt. But the move set back the programme another month.

Rather than being discouraged by the attack on Peenemünde, Hitler appeared to be even more enthused by the possibilities offered by the rocket. 'Hitler gave free reign to his imagination,' recalled Speer following a meeting at the Wolfsschanze on 25 August. 'He demanded an absolute minimum of 5,000 A-4 rockets within the shortest possible time … This will be retribution against England. With

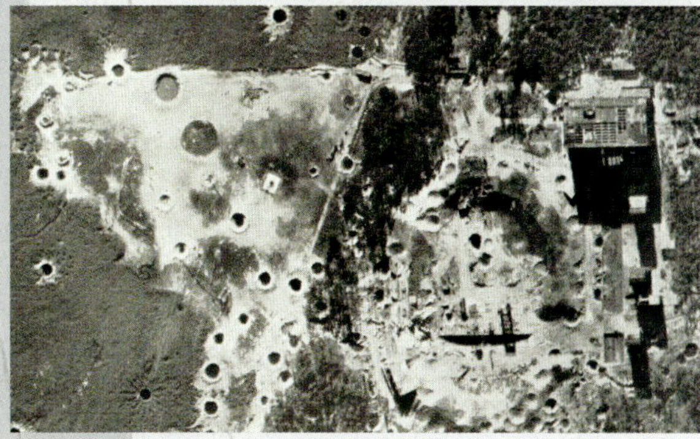

ABOVE *Test Stand VII after* Hydra. (HISTORIC MILITARY PRESS)

LEFT *The mother of Sergeant Robert Slaughter RAF at the grave of Flight Sergeant Norman Buchanan RAAF in Aabenraa Cemetery, Denmark. Buchanan and Slaughter were in the crew of a 49 Squadron Lancaster, JA691 coded EA-L, which was shot down during* Hydra. *There were no survivors.* (AUSTRALIAN WAR MEMORIAL; P09712.001)

this, we will force England to her knees. The use of this new weapon will make any enemy invasion impossible.'[8]

Much of the rocket testing was consequently moved to the Heidelager SS military training area at Blizna in south-east Poland. The mass production of the rockets, however, was to be located in the Harz Mountains in northern Germany. These moves enabled Himmler to take a leading role in the rocket programme, as he so earnestly desired, by ensuring that one of his officers, SS-Obergruppenführer und General der Waffen-SS Hans Kammler took charge of the construction work.

Testing did not begin at Blizna until 25 November. Consequently, this further hiatus in the A4 programme should be added to those initial five or so weeks lost after the Bomber Command attack. Operation *Hydra*, ▶

therefore, set back the development of the A4 by at least two months and, most importantly, just long enough to prevent it from dislocating the Allied invasion of Normandy ten months later. It must rate as one of the most effective bombing raids of the war.

The Luftwaffe areas at Peenemünde West, where the V1 flying bomb was being developed, had not been attacked on the night of 17/18 August, but that programme was also set back by the raid due to the evacuation of the forced labourers. So, manufacture of components for the V1 was undertaken to the north of the Harz Mountains, at the Volkswagen factory near the village of Fallersleben, where slave labour was again employed.

The damaged areas at Peenemünde were deliberately left in ruins in the hope that the Allied bombers would

ABOVE *The ruins of an air raid shelter near the Luftwaffe's test area at Peenemünde West.* (COURTESY OF GUNNAR KLACK)

regard the site as no longer of any interest; there were even efforts to paint some of the structures black to give the impression that they had been severely burnt. Some experimental work on the A4 did continue at Peenemünde and production of liquid oxygen was maintained there. But the raid effectively ended the rocket programme at Peenemünde upon which a staggering £25,000,000 had been spent since the beginning of the war. While the A4 would eventually deliver its warheads on London, all the years of research were dismantled in one single attack by conventional aircraft. Bomber Command's Arthur Harris wryly observed that: 'German threats of attack against this country by "secret weapons" thereafter became noticeably less specific as regards dates'.[9] ●

ABOVE LEFT *The remains of a V2 recovered from the site of the former experimental station at Blizna in Poland.* (DAMIAN PANKOWIEC/ SHUTTERSTOCK)

LEFT *A V2 rocket being prepared for launch at the Blizna test area.* (COURTESY OF THE PARK HISTORYCZNY BLIZNA)

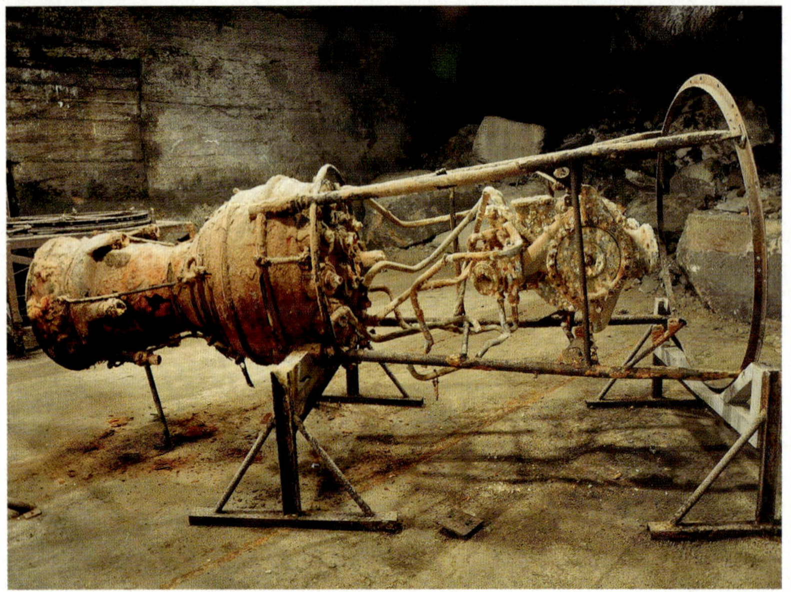

LEFT *The rusting remains of part of a V2 rocket engine, with its characteristic combustion chamber on the left, in the tunnels at Nordhausen. Both V1s and V2s were manufactured at this location, the tunnels of which had a total length of some twelve miles.* (COURTESY OF VINCENT VAN ZEIJST)

Crossbow Commences

THE ACTIVITIES AT PEENEMÜNDE HAD BEEN IDENTIFIED BY THE CENTRAL INTERPRETATION UNIT, BUT THE SEARCH WAS THEN ON TO FIND THE SITES FROM WHERE THE ROCKETS AND FLYING BOMBS WOULD BE FIRED AGAINST LONDON AND THE REST OF THE UK.

Flight Lieutenant Arthur H. 'Rufus' Riseley had trained as an Air Gunner and, as a sergeant, served throughout the Battle of Britain with the Bristol Blenheim-equipped 600 (City of London) Squadron. In 1941 Riseley was selected for pilot training, eventually being posted to 88 Squadron.

Flying Douglas Boston III and IIIA bombers, 88 Squadron moved to RAF Hartford Bridge, Hampshire, in August 1943. Along with 342 (Free French) Squadron, it formed 137 Wing of No.2 Group of the Second Tactical Air Force. From Hartford Bridge it carried out attacks on German coastal shipping and targets on the coast of Occupied Europe.

It was on just such a raid, on 16 August 1943, that thirty-seven aircraft from Nos. 88, 107 and 342 squadrons, led by Wing Commander G.R. England, were detailed to attack

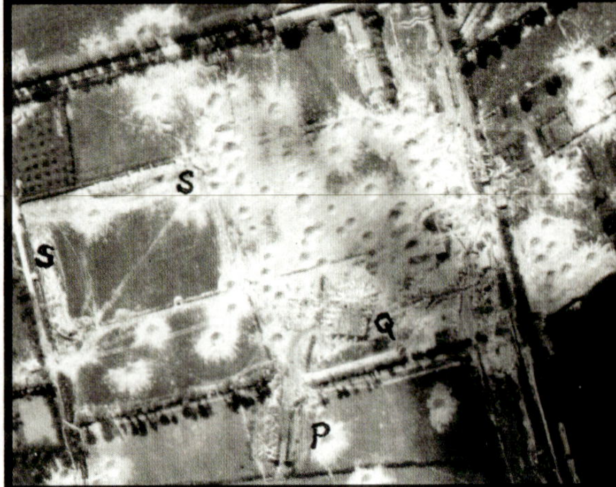

the armament and steel works at Denain, south-west of Valenciennes in northern France. The raid was a success, but as the aircraft headed for home, problems, and casualties, mounted. A total of two Typhoons and six Bostons were lost. One of the latter was Boston IIIA BZ359, flown by Flight Lieutenant Riseley and his crew.

For them, the trouble had started as they passed over Albert when the bomber's port engine was hit by anti-aircraft fire. Forced to slow down, and without the mutual support of the rest of the squadron, the damaged Boston was easy prey for Luftwaffe fighters. Soon hit in the starboard engine, Riseley was forced to put his aircraft down into a field east of Montorgueil, not far from Quesnoy-en-Artois. All four crew members were injured in the crash to a greater or lesser extent. Riseley, however, was only slightly bruised and was able to walk.

Turning his tunic inside out to hide his RAF wings, Riseley pulled his trouser legs down over his flying boots and set out to get aid for his wounded crew. Two local children guided him to a friendly farm where he arranged for his colleagues to be taken care of. Despite possessing only a smattering of schoolboy French, Riseley was able to make himself understood. As well as ensuring that his crew was as safe as they could be under the circumstances, Riseley soon fell into the hands of one of the local Resistance groups.

As his evader's journey back to the UK began, Riseley found himself at a village milliner's shop. There he heard a strange story. It was said that

the head of the local Gestapo had become a traitor. Riseley wanted to make contact with this man, who we are told was called Weiler, but who was most probably one Joseph Becker. A meeting was arranged for 3 September 1943. It was the beginning of what has been described as one of the strangest associations of the war.

Giant concrete Ramps

Such a meeting was potentially highly dangerous as it could well prove to be a trap, but it turned out to be quite the opposite. As remarkable as it seems, over what was described as 'a sumptuous champagne dinner', Weiler offered to take Riseley for a ride in his black saloon.

True to his word, Weiler duly took Riseley on a tour of the heavily defended area around Arras, the latter keeping notes of everything that he observed. Believing that he had vital information that should be passed back to London, but with no immediate prospect of getting to Britain himself, Riseley was helped by the Resistance who provided a carrier pigeon. So Riseley set up a pigeon post service detailing as best he could everything that he saw. He signed each message with his pre-war RAF Auxiliary number, 800360, to show that they were authentic.

Word then reached Riseley from another source about a secret

> "*After a while the track opened out and Riseley beheld the German's greatest secret – the beginning of the construction of giant concrete ramps from which would be launched the pilotless flying bombs.*"

establishment that Weiler had not told him about. This was in a heavily guarded wood to the south-west of Saint-Pol-sur-Ternoise. He learnt that work on the site at St Pol, near the village of Siracourt, had begun in July 1943. Riseley was determined to discover what was afoot. So, disguised as a French workman, he joined the crew of a lorry operating on the site.

Sat between two Frenchmen in the cab of the lorry, which was carrying supplies of timber and steel fittings to the secret facility, Riseley was seemingly able to enter the site without arousing suspicion. An account published in 1957 described what followed: 'Suddenly near the guarded area where Riseley knew the mystery work was going on, the lorry turned slap bang off the road and on to a cunningly-concealed track. At intervals stood guards, but they took little notice of the dirty, whiskered young "Frenchman" that Riseley had become. After a while the track opened out and Riseley beheld the German's greatest secret – the beginning of the construction of giant concrete ramps from which would be launched the pilotless flying bombs.'[1]

Across the site Riseley noted large slave labour gangs of Poles, Frenchmen and Hungarians at work, stripped to the waist. As he helped unload the supplies from the truck he tried to memorise as much as he could. He particularly noticed that

the secret installations were covered by camouflage nets making them all but impossible to detect from the air and he concluded it possible that no-one in the UK would be aware of what was happening in the forest.

Unsure what was being constructed at the secret site, but certain in his mind that it was something of great significance, Riseley decided that he must visit the location again. Despite the enormous risks, he repeated the previous method and once more entered the site, trying to observe more details of what was being built. Afterwards he drew detailed sketches of what he had seen, adding explanatory notes. He now needed to get this information back to Britain.

Flying bomb launch site

So effective had the Resistance network become, Riseley was smuggled out by the French group on a lobster boat called *Suzanne-Renée* which sailed out of Camaret-sur-Mer on 23 October 1943. The little ship's departure had been delayed by bad weather, but finally at 11.30 hours that day it put to sea with the remainder of the local fleet. Riseley and a group of other evaders were hidden under a pile of lobster pots in the ship's hold as *Suzanne-Renée* made its way past the German control at the entrance to the harbour. Fortunately, the control was not severe, a German sailor simply putting his head through the cabin door to check the fishing permit, and the men were not spotted.

Throughout the perilous thirty-six-hour crossing Riseley carried a very stale loaf under his arm. The inside of the loaf was hollowed out and it was there that he had stuffed his sketches and notes.

Suzanne-Renée remained with the other fishing vessels until late on the 23rd, at which point it broke away and set course for Penzance, where it arrived at 17.30 hours the following day. From there, the airmen were taken initially to Falmouth for a

much-needed meal, a bath and a new set of clothes. In due course, under open arrest the evaders were escorted on a train to London for interrogation and to continue their war.

Riseley's information, meanwhile, was passed onto British Intelligence. What he had seen was a bunker intended to be used as a bomb-proof storage facility and launch site for the V1 – exactly the type of structure the Interpreters had been searching for at Medmenham.

'A tiny cruciform shape'

Among those scrutinising photographs at Medmenham, in this case some of those of Peenemünde after the August raid, was one of the CIU's most notable characters, Constance Babington Smith. She later wrote about the moment on 1 December 1943 when she identified the ramps at Peenemünde as being

similar to those noted by Riseley: 'I pondered over the photographs and reviewed what I had found. There were four of these strange structures. Three of them looked very much like the sort of cranes that have a box for the operator and a long moveable arm. But the fourth seemed different and was the one that drew my attention most. It was evidently a sort of ramp banked up with earth – you could tell that from the shadow – supporting rails that inclined upwards towards the water's edge.'[2]

Looking at more photographs taken by Squadron Leader John Merrifield and his navigator, Flying Officer Whalley during their Mosquito flight over the Baltic on 28 November 1943, Babington Smith noticed something on the ramp which had not been on the earlier photograph: 'A tiny cruciform shape, set exactly on the

R.V. Jones had also been studying PRU photos of Peenemünde and had deduced that the pilotless craft would have to have a wingspan of less than 21 feet 9 inches, the width of an opening through which the complete weapon had to pass on its way to the launching ramp.

Such was the accumulation of knowledge, on 3 December Lord Cherwell, Churchill's scientific advisor, wrote the following to the Prime Minister who had been attending the Cairo Conference with President Roosevelt and the Chinese leader, Chiang Kai-shek: 'I have heard today that recent photographs at and near Peenemünde have disclosed sites resembling closely "ski" sites in ▶

lower end of the inclined rails – a midget aircraft actually in position for launching.'[3]

Pilotless aircraft

It was clear then, that there was a link between the once-secret testing site and the sites identified by the likes of Hollard and Riseley. What that link was, was equally obvious – the sites in the Pas-de-Calais were where Hitler' new V weapons would be stored, maintained or launched against London.

All the while, further reports of unusual structures being built in the Pas-de-Calais continued to be received by the various intelligence services. Such information was generally regarded with some caution, for the reliability of the sources could not be ascertained. The only certain knowledge was that obtained by aerial photography – the camera never lies.

LEFT *One of the major V1 installations attacked by Allied bombers was that located at Brécourt near Cherbourg. Though originally intended to be used for the V2, the facility, known to the Germans as Wasserwerk II, was converted to become one of four major V1 launch facilities in Northern France, its launch ramp being directed towards Bristol and Cardiff. This picture was taken on 12 July 1944, after the site was captured by American troops.* (USNHHC)

LEFT *Another view of the launch ramp of Wasserwerk II at Brécourt. Note the camouflage nets strung over the top.* (HISTORIC MILITARY PRESS)

BELOW *A member of an RAF and RAAF party examines the damage wrought by Allied bombing on a 'ski site' in northern France.* (AUSTRALIAN WAR MEMORIAL; 133033)

France, of which there are now sixty to one hundred under construction. 'Since they showed gentle ramps – one with a pilotless aircraft on it – and since we know quite definitely that successful experiments with pilotless aircraft are being made in that region, it seems almost certain that the "ski" sites are intended for this weapon. The aircraft have a span of about twenty feet and it is reckoned that they might carry a bomb weighing about two tons. The speed is probably something over four hundred miles per hour, and the height at which they have hitherto been flown is about six thousand feet.' The description of the launch ramps as ski sites was because of their resemblance from above to a ski laid on its side.

The feared, if undetermined, threat of secret weapons being directed against London now had a solid form. As Cherwell added, somewhat unnecessarily, in his message to Churchill, 'the launching of 1,000 of these aircraft, could produce very unpleasant concentrated effects'.

The immediate effect was to concentrate minds on stopping the pilotless aircraft before they were launched. The Air Ministry's Director of Intelligence (Operations) actually painted an even more unpleasant estimation of the potential destructive power of these weapons than Cherwell, stating that the layout and storage arrangements suggested that the enemy's intention was to make a concentrated attack. Rapid and

> *"The description of the launch ramps as ski sites was because of their resemblance from above to a ski laid on its side."*

simultaneous fire from a likely 100 sites could, he concluded, deliver 2,000 tons of high explosive on London within the space of twenty-four hours. This was the equivalent of the bombload dropped on Hamburg which had destroyed the city – and the Germans would continue to bombard London for as long as they were able to manufacture the weapons.

The staff at Medmenham strained their eyes, and every nerve, in an effort to locate the launching ramps and, now well aware of what they were searching for, sixty-nine sites had been identified in northern France by the middle of December. The next step was to decide the best method of bombing the so-called ski sites into oblivion.

ABOVE *The battered Château de Bosmelet near Auffay in Upper Normandy. The Château was badly damaged in 1944 when the Allies bombed the adjacent V1 launch site, Feuerstellung 690. The launch ramp is believed to be the structure marked 'P'. This photograph was taken from about 15,000ft by Lieutenant Colonel John S. Blyth who flew various Spitfire Mk.XIs on his V weapon missions. At the time, Lieutenant Colonel Blyth was flying with the 14th Squadron of the USAAF's 7th PRG based at Mount Farm, Oxfordshire.* (WITH THE KIND PERMISSION OF SCOTT BLYTH)

LEFT *Also taken by Lieutenant Colonel Blyth, this image, dated 7 July 1944, shows the V1 launch site at Flers, France – Feuerstellung 122. Once again, the letter 'P' indicates the position of the launch ramp.* (WITH THE KIND PERMISSION OF SCOTT BLYTH)

RIGHT *Bombs fall onto a smoke shrouded target from a Bomber Command Lancaster during a raid on V1 Installations in the Pas de Calais.* (AUSTRALIAN WAR MEMORIAL; SUK12490)

Mission number 164

In November 1943, the Bodyline Committee had become the Crossbow Committee. Though *Crossbow* was the codename for all operations against all elements of the German long-range weapons programme, its first major effort was to be against the ski sites of what would soon to be called the V1.

By the third week of December, the identified total of ski sites had risen to seventy-five, and senior Air Ministry officials decided to begin bombing the sites as soon as possible, using tactical air forces then being marshalled for the Normandy landings. The problem that the air leaders had to solve was not only to determine what to strike and how to strike it, but also how often to strike. One well-placed 2,000lb delayed-action bomb could do more damage than twenty-five 500lb bombs scattered indiscriminately from a high altitude. On the other hand, the more bombs dropped on a given area, the higher the probability that at least one would find its mark.

LEFT *This aerial reconnaissance photograph was taken whilst a V1 was in position on the launch ramp of this unidentified Feuerstellung in northern France.* (HISTORIC MILITARY PRESS)

LEFT *Evidence of Allied bomb damage can be seen on this V1 launch ramp of Feuerstellung 618, which is located in woodland between the villages of Journy and Neuville. The pasture on the far side of the track to the right of the ramp is littered with bomb craters.* (HISTORIC MILITARY PRESS)

LEFT *The V1 'ski site' at Val Ygot near the town of Ardouval, known to the Germans as Feuerstellung 685, has survived reasonably intact, albeit having been badly damaged by Allied bombing – so much so, in fact, that it never became operational. This pile of concrete is the flattened remains of the V1 reception building.* (HISTORIC MILITARY PRESS)

LEFT *The result of another near miss or direct hit at Feuerstellung 685. This structure is the main assembly workshop, half of which has been demolished by bombing.* (HISTORIC MILITARY PRESS)

Analysts working for the RAF tried to estimate the number of attacks and the tonnage of bombs needed to do serious damage to a ski site.

On the basis of early results, the RAF concluded that medium bombers operating at lower altitudes were ineffective against V weapon sites, or *Noball* targets as they were also known. On 15 December 1943, the British Chiefs of Staff decided to draw the US into the *Crossbow* offensive, by asking the Americans to use their Eighth Air Force's heavy bombers to help attack the ski sites. The Americans agreed, but because of bad weather it was not until Christmas Eve that the Eighth Air Force made its first *Crossbow* attack.

More than 1,300 aircraft participated in Mission 164, the largest Eighth Air Force operation to that point. Six hundred and seventy Boeing B-17s and Consolidated B-24 Liberators, escorted by Republic P-47 Thunderbolts, North American P-51 Mustangs and Lockheed P-38 Lightnings, dropped 1,700 tons of explosives on twenty-three ski sites. Despite the massive scale of the attack, only three of the twenty-three ski sites were completely destroyed.

The bombing of the ski sites was relentless, though there was no increase in the success rate. This was commented on by Churchill on 10 January 1944, after being shown some post-operational reconnaissance photographs. 'What really surprises me about the photographs,' the Prime Minister remarked in a note to the Chief of the Air Staff, Sir Charles Portal, 'is how little harm we have been able to do with ordinary explosive bombs. Are you attacking all camps and hutments where labour may be accumulated for constructing these places? The photographs certainly show that a liberal drenching with mustard gas would make all work, especially firing, very difficult.'

Surprisingly, the use of chemical weapons was a subject that was not often entirely dismissed, as will be seen later. ●

NOTES

1. Quoted in the *Sunday Pictorial* of 14 July 1957.
2. Constance Babington Smith, *Evidence in Camera, The Story of Photographic Intelligence in the Second World War* (Penguin, London, 1957), pp.205-7.
3. ibid.

A Big Job for Tall Boys

AS THE GERMANS BEGAN TO BUILD MASSIVE STRUCTURES FOR THEIR LONG-RANGE BOMBARDMENT WEAPONS, THE RAF'S ORDINARY BOMBS WERE FOUND TO BE INEFFECTIVE. IT WAS A BIG PROBLEM WHICH REQUIRED A BIG SOLUTION – THE EARTHQUAKE BOMB.

T he ski sites were not the only long-range weapons facilities that were targeted by the Allies in 1943 and 1944. A number of very large secret facilities were being built at various locations in the Pas-de-Calais and Normandy. One of these was in the Forest of Éperlecques, near Watten in northern France. Though it and the other 'heavy' sites' true purpose was undetermined, as Lord Cherwell noted, 'if it is worth the enemy's while to go to all the trouble of building them it would seem worth ours to destroy them'.

BELOW *The Blockhaus d'Éperlecques, near Watten, photographed by a de Havilland Mosquito of 540 Squadron on 23 July 1944.* (HISTORIC MILITARY PRESS)

The site in Éperlecques forest had been selected by Dornberger as early as December 1942 for deployment of the A4. Its forest location would help conceal if from the air (or so it was hoped), it was just 1.5 miles from the nearest railway station, which was at Watten, and a mile from the nearest railway line. It was also conveniently close to main roads and a canal. The site was supplied by three electric grid

lines and all three would have to be cut to prevent the site from operating. It was designed to accommodate 108 V2 rockets and the personnel to launch them at an expected rate of at least thirty-six per day. The facility was to also incorporate a liquid oxygen plant and a bomb-proof railway siding to allow missiles and supplies to be delivered direct from production facilities in Germany.

Design of the Éperlecques site, codenamed Kraftwerk Nord West and more commonly simply referred to as Watten, began in January 1943, the plans of which were completed and authorised by Hitler on 25 March. Slave and PoW labour – some 3-4,000 men worked round the clock on twelve-hour shifts – under the infamous Organisation Todt was used to build the site which was expected to be operational in November 1943.

Despite the hope that the activities in the forest would go undetected, CIU staff had spotted unusual activity in the area as early as May 1943, but an attack

ABOVE *An aerial reconnaissance photograph of the Watten bunker after Allied bombing. Note the large Tallboy craters.* (NARA)

RIGHT *A Halifax pictured during an attack on the bunker at Siracourt on 22 June 1944. Completed in 1943, this structure was intended as a 'giant launch shelter' for V1s. The bombing, which included at least two further raids, forced the Germans to abandon the facility before a single V1 was launched.* (HISTORIC MILITARY PRESS)

was not ordered until August. This was because Sir Malcolm McAlpine, the chairman of the construction company Sir Robert McAlpine, suggested that to inflict the most permanent damage on the huge buildings, the site should be attacked while the concrete was still setting.

Consequently, it was on the evening of 27 August 1943, that 224 Boeing B-17 Flying Fortresses of the Eighth Air Force attacked Watten on Mission 87. It was claimed that

187 of the bombers hit the target; four B-17s were lost. The damage inflicted on the site was significant. The fortified railway station at the northern part of the bunker was heavily damaged as the concrete had just been poured.

Walter Dornberger subsequently wrote that the site, after the attack, was just a 'devastated heap of concrete, steel, struts and wooden boards. The concrete hardened out and after a few days the structure was ▶

> *"Walter Dornberger subsequently wrote that the site, after the attack, was just a 'devastated heap of concrete, steel, struts and wooden boards."*

beyond repair. All we could do was to put on a roof and use it for another purpose' – just as McAlpine had calculated.

The raid was a tremendous success, with the only disappointment being that, as with the Peenemünde raid, the bombing killed and wounded hundreds of labour workers. Watten was attacked again by the Americans on 7 September, leaving the site, according to the interpreters at Medmenham, 'a desolate heap'.

La Coupole

Following the destruction of Watten, another site had to be found for the A4. The place chosen was in a disused quarry around nine miles

to the south-east of Watten near St Omer. This was to be the Coupole d'Helfaut-Wizernes, often referred to simply as La Coupole, to which the Germans allocated the codenames Bauvorhaben 21 and Schotterwerk Nordwest.

Work on converting the quarry into a missile storage depot, where V2 rockets would be housed in tunnels bored into the chalk hillside before being transported to Watten for launching, had already been taken in hand. It was an obvious step to turn the Wizernes site into a combined storage and launch facility and, following a meeting with Speer and Franz Xaver Dorsch, the chief engineer of the Todt Organisation, on 30 September 1943, Hitler agreed to Dorsch's plans to create a massive subterranean structure.

Dorsch planned to use a million tons of concrete to construct an impenetrable dome (the Coupole or cupola) on the hillside overlooking the quarry and a series of connecting tunnels. About 7 kilometres of underground galleries would be excavated beneath the dome and inside the chalk hillside. The dimensions of the dome were gigantic; 71 metres in diameter, 5 metres thick and with a weight of 55 tons. The tunnels under the dome would accommodate workshops, storerooms, fuel supplies, a liquid oxygen manufacturing plant, generators, barracks and a hospital. The intention was that the rockets would be serviced in this sheltered chamber, then hauled out into the open along two concrete tunnels (named Gretchen and Gustav) and launched at London.

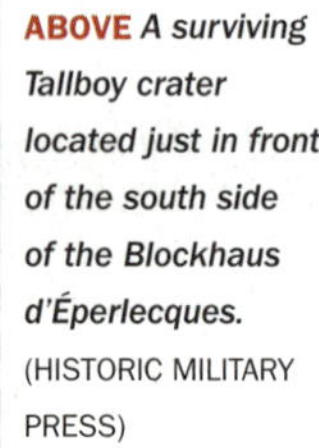

ABOVE *A surviving Tallboy crater located just in front of the south side of the Blockhaus d'Éperlecques.* (HISTORIC MILITARY PRESS)

ABOVE RIGHT *A view of the south side of the Blockhaus d'Éperlecques, or Watten bunker, showing damage caused by a Tallboy bomb. This picture was taken during an RAF survey in 1951.* (HISTORIC MILITARY PRESS)

MIDDLE LEFT *This commemorative panel on the D222 road, less than a mile west of the village of Éperlecques, overlooks the area in which a 640 Squadron Halifax, Mk.III NA578, crashed on 25 August 1944. Flown by Pilot Officer Cyril White, it was part of a force of 161 aircraft despatched to bomb various V weapon sites in northern France. It is believed to have fallen victim to anti-aircraft fire.* (HISTORIC MILITARY PRESS)

The enemy activity at Wizernes was detected by the CIU in August 1943, but it was not until March 1944 that it was regarded as part of the secret weapons programme and was added to the list of *Crossbow* targets. From then onwards, Wizernes was attacked sixteen times by the Allies, in which RAF and USAAF bombers dropped 4,260 tons of bombs.

It was found, however, that Wizernes was so powerfully constructed that conventional bombs had little effect on the massive bunker. Something out of the ordinary was required and this was found in the 'Tallboy', or Bomb, Medium Capacity, 12,000lbs. Designed by Barnes Wallis, each Tallboy comprised almost three tons of explosive in an aerodynamically refined armour-piercing casing. It could blast its way through five metres of reinforced concrete – the ideal bomb to drop on the likes of Wizernes. So powerful were these 'earthquake' bombs, even near misses might either damage side walls or undermine foundations, and severe shocks might disrupt sensitive equipment inside.

To be able to penetrate the earth or hardened targets without breaking apart, the casing of the Tallboy had to be strong. Each was cast in one piece of high-tensile steel that would enable it to survive the impact before detonation. At the same time, to achieve the penetration required, Wallis designed the Tallboy to be very aerodynamic so that, when dropped from a great height, it would reach a much higher terminal velocity than traditional bomb designs.

The only squadron whose aircraft were adapted to take the Tallboy bombs at this time was 617 Squadron. These weapons were not to be dropped in the usual Bomber Command fashion of area bombing at night. There were three main reasons for this. The first was that these specially-built bombs were in short supply and could not be wasted in area bombing. Secondly, their destructive power was so enormous that they had to be delivered with precision, which meant that they had to be dropped in daylight. The third reason was their cost of manufacture.

It was actually against the Kraftwerk Nord West at Watten that 617 Squadron started its Tallboy operations late in the afternoon of 19 June 1944. This attack was followed by raids on Wizernes on 20, 22 and 24 June. The obvious dangers of operating in daylight became apparent on the raid of 24 June, as Flight Sergeant Gerry Hobbs, the Wireless Operator of Lancaster DV403, coded KC-G, recalled:

'In a cloudless sky we climbed over the Channel and heading towards the target the English coastline could still be seen. We were on our straight and level bombing run when two Flak bursts hit us and both port engines were set on fire. The flight engineer was killed instantly and but for the huge bomb beneath us the

RIGHT Groundcrew and armourers prepare to load a Lancaster with a 12,000lb Tallboy bomb. The aircraft in this picture is a 460 Squadron RAAF example. (AUSTRALIAN WAR MEMORIAL; P00878.002)

BELOW Three bomb trailers are pictured carrying 12,000lb Tallboy bombs waiting to be loaded into Lancasters of 9 Squadron. (AUSTRALIAN WAR MEMORIAL; P04387.004)

BOTTOM A view of the south-west corner of the Blockhaus d'Éperlecques at Watten. Note the Tallboy damage on the roof to the right, as well as further bomb damage on the left. (HISTORIC MILITARY PRESS)

Flak may have claimed more victims. The navigator, after checking the flight engineer, assisted the pilot in trying to extinguish the fires but to no avail and the pilot ordered him to jump. I was the wireless operator and I returned to the intercom when I saw the engines alight, to hear the pilot call, "Abracadabra, jump, jump", which was our pre-arranged signal to abandon aircraft.

'There was a split second of panic whilst deciding whether to remove my flying helmet, but I took it off and then the drill took over and I moved aft to the rear door. I clipped on my parachute pack … climbed over the main spar and met the mid-upper gunner who shouted in my ear that the rear was alight and that we couldn't get out that way. Forward again over the main spar and now the aircraft was shuddering violently. I stepped over the flight engineer, just as the pilot was leaving his seat. He didn't see us, and I didn't distract him, but I remember releasing his oxygen tube, as he made his way down to the front hatch. I saw him checking his harness and then I passed out through lack of oxygen.'[1]

The next thing Hobbs remembered was regaining consciousness in a cornfield surrounded by German soldiers and French civilians. The pilot, Flight Lieutenant J.A. Edward, did not survive.

Poison gas warheads

Though the *Crossbow* operations were virtually continuous, there was still concern that the Germans would be able to launch their V weapons against London and possibly the ports along the English south coast where the D-Day flotillas would assemble. There was, strangely, a follow up to Churchill's suggestion of using chemical weapons. There was concern that the Germans

LEFT This low-level oblique reconnaissance photograph of the V2 assembly and storage facility at Wizernes was taken prior to the successful attack on it by 617 Squadron, using Tallboy bombs, on 17 July 1944. The 1-million-ton concrete dome covering the underground workings lies at the head of the quarry, with a 100-foot high hammerhead crane positioned in front of it. (HISTORIC MILITARY PRESS)

LEFT The entrance tunnel to La Coupole as it appears to the visitor today. The tunnel you see here was originally constructed to take a railway spur. The massive dome can be seen top right. During 617 Squadron's attack on 17 July 1944, one Tallboy caused the concrete dome to shift out of alignment, whilst two others had the effect of causing a roof collapse and blocking the entrance. (HISTORIC MILITARY PRESS)

LEFT An oblique aerial reconnaissance photograph of Wasserwerk 1 at Siracourt taken after Allied bombing. The RAF's attack on this site on 25 June 1944, involved the Lancasters of 617 Squadron which dropped Tallboy bombs. (HISTORIC MILITARY PRESS)

might arm their new weapons with poison gas warheads. The prospect of such weapons landing amidst the Operation *Overlord* assembly areas filled the Allied Supreme Commander, General Eisenhower, with dread. The USAAF and Bomber Command were ordered to draw up plans to retaliate in kind against a pre-selected number of German cities.

Eisenhower was correct in his concerns about the possibility of the V weapons being deployed against his invasion forces. Hitler believed that the Allied amphibious assault would take place across the narrowest part of the English Channel, the Dover Strait, to land in the Pas-de-Calais. It was also in this region of France that the majority of the V weapon launching sites were erected. Hitler saw this region of France as being the 'decisive' battle ground and ordered the German Fifteenth Army, which guarded the French coast, to be substantially reinforced.

Crossbow missions continued apace to try and prevent the V weapons being deployed. In March 1944, 2,800 sorties were undertaken against related sites in which 4,150 tons of bombs were dropped. In April this rose to 4,150 sorties and 7,500 tons of bombs. Yet no clear picture of exactly how much permanent damage to the various sites had so far emerged. In fact, the bombing of the 'heavy' sites had caused Hitler to concede to Dornberger's suggestion of mobile launch sites, and when the Allied ground forces overran the heavy sites after D-Day, they commented on the very obvious damage that the Tallboys had inflicted on these huge structures.

What was certain from the PRU photographs, on the other hand, was that the Germans were still working feverishly on the launch sites which could only mean that production of the weapons was in progress. It might well be, therefore, that the Germans were close to deployment of the new weapons. This was shown in a report to the Joint Chiefs of Staff from the Air Ministry on 16 March 1944, in which they believed that the new weapons might be in use at the end of the month. So, in addition to the *Crossbow* offensive, defensive measures had to be considered. ●

NOTE

1   See Mark Postlethwaite with Jim Shortland, *Dambusters in Focus, A Photographic Album of 617 'Dambuster' Squadron at War 1943-1945* (Red Kite, Walton on Thames, 2007), p.86.

Defending Britain's Skies

WITH CONSIDERABLE ACCUMULATED KNOWLEDGE OF THE NATURE AND LIKELY CAPABILITIES OF THE GERMAN MISSILES, A PLAN TO DEFEND BRITAIN AGAINST THE EXPECTED ATTACKS WAS DEVISED – BUT NO ONE REALLY KNEW WHAT WOULD HAPPEN WHEN HITLER'S NEW WEAPONS BEGAN TO FALL.

T he RAF's Fighter Command, which had defended Britain's skies throughout the Battle of Britain and the Blitz, was disbanded in November 1943. The aerial threat once posed by the Luftwaffe had considerably receded and the RAF and USAAF had turned their attention to offensive operations in preparation for the invasion of Europe. With most fighter squadrons being incorporated into the newly-formed Allied Expeditionary Air Force, the man who took command of the Air Defence of Great Britain (ADGB), Air Chief Marshal Sir Roderick Hill, had just thirty-three squadrons at his disposal – less than half of what had been considered necessary for the defence of the UK at the end of 1941.

From the very start of his tenure Hill was aware of the growing body of evidence which indicated that the Germans were preparing to launch deadly new weapons upon Britain.

BELOW *Appearing as black dots, barrage balloons stretch as far as the eye can seen in this view of part of the barrage that extended across much of southern England in the summer of 1944. It was described 'as the greatest balloon barrage to be placed in the air'.* (AUSTRALIAN WAR MEMORIAL; SUK12862)

All that Hill knew for certain was that these included both a long-range rocket of some kind and also some form of flying bomb, or pilotless aircraft. He was told that the latter, seen as the most imminent threat, flew at a speed of between 230 and 400 miles an hour and had a range of about 160 miles. He was also advised to assume that the attack upon the United Kingdom would amount to as many as two missiles an hour from each of 100 or so launch sites. The attacks, he was informed, might begin as early as February 1944.

These estimates were so broad that there was little Hill could put in place to deal with these missiles. ▶

Nevertheless, he viewed the situation quite pragmatically: 'I took as my point of departure the fundamental proposition that a pilotless aircraft was still an aircraft, and therefore vulnerable to the same basic methods of attack. Of course, as there was no crew, such an aircraft could not be made to crash by killing the pilot; on the other hand, it would be incapable of retreat or evasion, except, perhaps, to a very limited extent.'

A plan to counter the threat from these, the V1s, was approved by the Chiefs of Staff in January 1944, with the likely targets being London, the Solent and Bristol. London was to be protected by a belt of 528 heavy and 804 light anti-aircraft guns sited on a line south of Redhill–Maidstone–Thames estuary. In front of the gun-belt was to be the fighter zone in which the aircraft were to maintain a twenty-four-hour watch up to the French coast. A searchlight belt of nineteen batteries (456 lights), in front of the range limit of the gun-belt, was to co-operate with the fighters by illuminating the flying bombs at night. Behind the gun-belt was to be a barrage of 480 cable-carrying balloons as a final check. The reason for placing London's defence deployment well inland was to reduce enemy jamming of the radar equipment, as well as to allow the RAF's fighters the maximum area for manoeuvre.

To protect the Solent area, the Isle of Wight air defences were to be re-adjusted; and for Bristol a similar lay-out to that of London was planned on a smaller scale, with the gun-belt to the north of Shaftesbury.

ABOVE RAF personnel raising a balloon barrage. As the V1 campaign unfolded, increasing numbers of barrage balloons were used - so much so that by 10 August 1944, a concentration of 2,003 balloons had been deployed, this being the largest number ever assembled. (HISTORIC MILITARY PRESS)

RIGHT A 40mm Bofors gun crew pictured prior to the V weapon campaign. By 10 August 1944, no less than 1,312 examples of this anti-aircraft gun had been deployed against the flying bomb onslaught. (HISTORIC MILITARY PRESS)

> "Guns and searchlights would provide the next line of defence and would become the first line of defence if at any time the state of the weather or any other factor prevented the fighters from operating."

The total stock of flying bombs amassed by the Germans by June 1944 was estimated to be between 8,000 and 14,000, with production likely to be around 1,000 to 1,500 units a month. Of the known launching sites, seventy-two were observed to be actively in use, and it was seen that many of the sites damaged by bombing could be quickly repaired. Priority was therefore given to bombing the supply communications and storage depots as being the most likely method of reducing the scale of attack.

What did alarm Hill, though, was that if the missiles would be capable of the maximum speed suspected, the existing fighter aircraft would prove incapable of intercepting them. Hill was also concerned that his aircraft, chasing missiles across Britain, would be exposed to friendly fire from the anti-aircraft batteries.

Much then depended upon early warning being given to the fighter squadrons. Hill found that the existing radar chain stations believed that they could detect pilotless aircraft in the same way as they detected ordinary aircraft. They also thought that they would be able to differentiate between piloted and pilotless aircraft by 'track behaviour' – in other words, the characteristics of their flight as interpreted by the radar responses. It was also expected that the members of the Royal Observer Corps would be able to recognise pilotless aircraft by their appearance and the noise they made.

As described in detail a little further on, the Germans' V weapons assault upon the UK began on the night of 12/13 June 1944. How well Hill, and the man in charge of Anti-Aircraft Command, General Sir Frederick Pile, had prepared for this event, would now be tested.

The defence lines

The first line of defence against the V1 was to be Allied fighters. 'For the defence of London,' noted Hill in a subsequent report, 'the arrangement envisaged in both plans was that whenever an attack in daylight seemed imminent, fighters of No.11 Group would patrol at 12,000 feet on three patrol lines, 20 miles off the coast between Beachy Head and Dover,

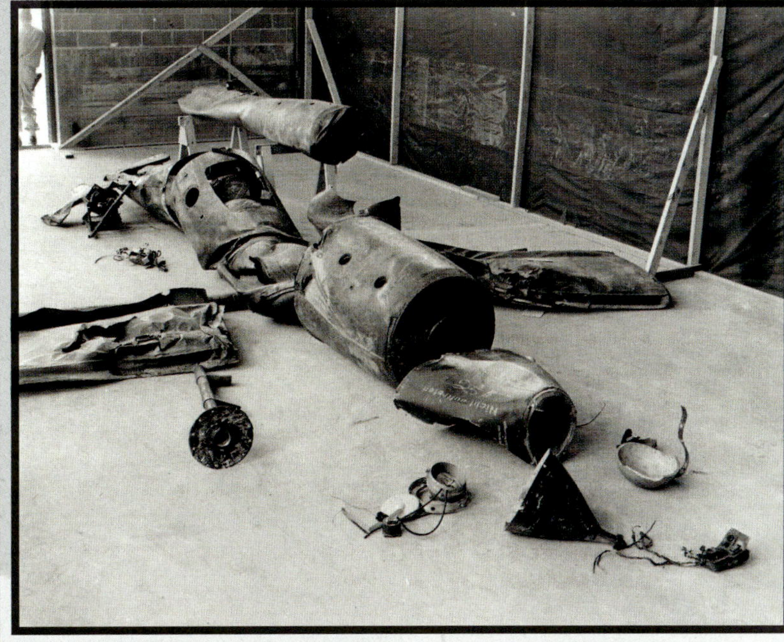

MIDDLE RIGHT *A barrage balloon cable is pictured wound tightly around the wing of a V1 which was brought down in the summer of 1944. The cable was fitted with a 'double parachute link', this being a device which automatically severed the cable near its top and bottom. Parachutes then opened at each end of this portion with the object of stalling the flying bomb.* (AUSTRALIAN WAR MEMORIAL; SUK12864)

BELOW *This is stated to be a view of the site where the first flying bomb was brought down by a barrage balloon. The crater is in the background and a demolished barn in the foreground.* (AUSTRALIAN WAR MEMORIAL; SUK12862)

over the coastline between Newhaven and Dover, and between Haywards Heath and Ashford respectively. Once an attack had begun, additional aircraft would patrol these lines at 6,000 feet …

'At Bristol and the Solent, the facts of geography promised a longer warning and more room to manoeuvre as well as a lighter scale of attack. Consequently, I did not propose to fly standing patrols for the defence of those places. Should attacks appear imminent, however, fighters would be held ready to intercept by normal methods.'[1]

At night a different scheme was to be used. Under this plan, fighters would patrol under the control of radar stations. If necessary, these could be reinforced by aircraft directed by the respective Sector control.

Guns and searchlights would provide the next line of defence and would become the first line of defence if at any time the state of the weather or any other factor prevented the fighters from operating. For the defence of London, Pile originally proposed massing 400 heavy anti-aircraft guns in folds and hollows on the southern slopes of the North Downs, where their radar equipment would be liable to the minimum of interference from 'jamming' by the enemy. Added to this were some 346 light anti-aircraft guns which were deployed largely on searchlight sites, of which there were 216 at the start of the V1 campaign.

Elsewhere, in front of Bristol were ninety-six heavy and 216 light guns, with 132 searchlights. Thirty-two heavy, 242 light, and a smaller number of searchlights defended the Solent. When Operation *Overlord* began, ▶

however, every possible gun was needed in France and the numbers left available for the defence of southern Britain were drastically reduced. This left London defended by 438 guns and the Solent by just 138 guns. There were, in addition to these anti-aircraft batteries, 560 smaller-calibre weapons ranged along the south coast in the form of 192 40mm Bofors and 368 20mm guns. To man these, the RAF

Regiment was employed as well as the Royal Navy (including DEMS – Defensively Equipped Merchant Ship – personnel) the Royal Marines and even men from the Army training camps and anti-aircraft tanks of the Royal Armoured Corps.

The third line of defence for London was that of balloons. This took the form of a permanent barrage of 480 balloons immediately behind the guns on the high ground between Cobham in Kent in the east and Limpsfield in the west.

The move south

During the next twenty-four hours the Germans launched over 200 V1s. Of this number, 144 crossed the coasts of Kent and Sussex and seventy-three reached the Greater London area. Thirty-three flying bombs were brought down by the defences, but eleven of these came down in the built-up areas of the capital.

The defenders in and around London continued to fire at the incoming V1s – though this soon led to its own problems, as Pile himself later noted: 'For three nights the guns

in London fired at those targets which had penetrated the primary defences, but after that they were restricted since it was clear that it was better to allow the flying bombs a chance of passing the more densely populated parts of the Capital rather than to shoot them down into it.'

Hill and Pile had already planned to mount most of the anti-aircraft guns along the North Downs but had expected a period of notice before the V1s started dropping, during which time they would be able to move their guns from the London area. Now they had to move quickly. This redeployment took just five days to complete.

Meanwhile, the first line of defence, the fighters of No.11 Group (in the form of Hawker Tempest Vs, Supermarine Spitfire XIVs, XIIs, and IXs, Hawker Typhoons, and, at night, de Havilland Mosquitoes), were bringing down around 30 per cent of all the V1s which crossed or approached the coast. On 16 June 1944, Hill issued orders defining the area which the fighters could patrol as being the Channel and the land between the coast and the southern limit of the gun-belt. The aircraft were prohibited from passing over the gun-belt except when actually pursuing a V1.

It was soon found that in good weather the fighters were much more successful than the guns, which were badly hampered by the fact that the flying bombs flew between 2,000 and 3,000 feet, which was too high to be effectively engaged by the light

anti-aircraft guns and too low for the heavy 3.7-inch guns. On the other hand, when the weather was bad, poor visibility hampered the fighters, and in these conditions the guns were the more effective weapon.

Accordingly, Hill set out strict rules of engagement. These were that in very good weather the guns should abstain from firing in order to give the fighters complete freedom of action. Conversely, when the weather was bad, the guns would have freedom of

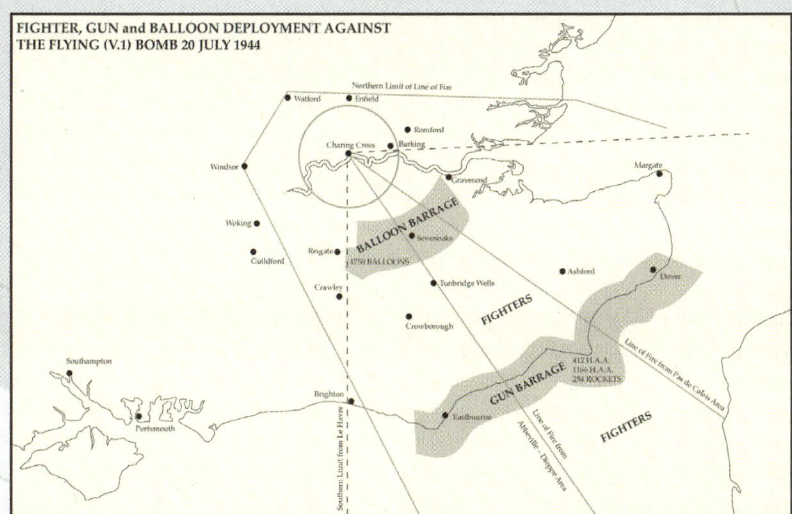

To undertake this repositioning exercise was no small task, for 'the move involved the transport of 23,000 men and women, and 30,000 tons of ammunition, also the laying of 3,000 miles of inter-battery cable'. The benefits, though, were almost immediately apparent. Assisted by the arrival from the United States of new radar sets designed to work successfully

LEFT *A map showing the revised general scheme for defence against the V1 that was agreed at HQ Fighter Command on 13 July 1944.* (HISTORIC MILITARY PRESS)

action and no fighters would be used. In what he described as 'middling' weather fighters would operate in front of the gun-belt and enter it only when pursuing a V1. When a fighter entered the gun-belt for this purpose the guns would, of course, withhold their fire, otherwise the guns inside the belt would be free to fire up to 8,000 feet. The guns were not permitted to fire outside the prescribed gun-belt. The only exception to this was that the light guns that were linked to the communications network might open fire on targets they could see, provided no fighters were about.

Adjusting the Defences

As the V1 campaign gathered pace, it was soon realised that the defensive plan could be refined. Consequently, at a meeting held at Fighter Command's headquarters on 13 July it was decided to move the gun-belt to the coast. 'The fighter pilots would be able to identify the position of the gun-belt by the coast-line,' notes one official history, 'radar sets would be free of inland interference, and enemy jamming methods were not apparently being used; flying bombs brought down by the guns would probably fall into the sea instead of on land.

'The move to the new gun-belt, between Cuckmere Haven (west of Eastbourne) and St. Margaret's Bay (east of Dover) began on the 14th July, and was completed in four days. The mobile heavy batteries were largely replaced by static mixed batteries for which platforms had to be extemporised out of steel rails, sleepers and ballast.'[2]

ABOVE *A general view of the main part of a US SCR-584 radar unit. All the operational equipment was housed within the caravan, although the M-9 director and power generators were separate.* (NOAA)

at high angles of sight,[3] and which one historian notes were supplied 'in response to a special request by Churchill',[4] the success rate against the V1 rose from 17 per cent in the first week to 55 per cent. in the fourth week.[5]

Despite such extensive defences, and their increasing success, V1s were still getting through, causing casualties and creating fear, and the V2 rockets had yet to make their appearance. The battle against Hitler's Vengeance weapons still had to be won. ●

LEFT *The flight path of a V1 pictured at night. The original caption to this image states that it shows 'the path of the flying bomb at night; the bomb is being held in a powerful searchlight ready for AA gunners to go into action'.* (HISTORIC MILITARY PRESS)

NOTES

1 For Hill's report, see John Grehan and Martin Mace, *Defending Britain's Skies, 1940-1945* (Pen & Sword, Barnsley, 2014), pp.195-282.

2 Quoted in *Stopping Hitler: An Official Account of How Britain Planned to Defend Itself in the Second World War* (Frontline Books, Barnsley, 2017).

3 These were examples of the SCR-584 radar, which was an automatic-tracking microwave radar developed by the MIT Radiation Laboratory. It was one of the most advanced ground-based radars of its era and became one of the primary gun-laying radars used worldwide well into the 1950s.

4 'Automation's Finest Hour: Radar and System Integration in World War II', a paper by David A. Mindell.

5 See *Stopping Hitler: An Official Account of How Britain Planned to Defend Itself in the Second World War*.

Diver! Diver! Diver! Diver!

ON 6 JUNE 1944, ALLIED FORCES LANDED IN NORMANDY. THE GERMANS RESPONDED A WEEK LATER WITH THE OPENING OF THEIR *VERGELTUNGSWAFFEN* WEAPON CAMPAIGN AGAINST THE UNITED KINGDOM.

The original date on which the *Vergeltungswaffen* weapons attack would commence against the UK had originally been set for Hitler's birthday, 20 April. This had proven to be impracticable, and so a new date had to be set. The order to start the campaign had been signed by the Führer in May, and General Keitel, the Commander-in-Chief of the Wehrmacht, issued the following instructions:

'The Führer has ordered [that] the long-range bombardment of England will begin in the middle of June. The exact date will be sent by Commander-in-Chief West [Feldmarschall Albert Kesselring] who will also control the bombardment with the help of LXV Army Corps and 3rd Air Fleet … The main target; London.

'The bombardment will open like a thunderclap by night … combined with bombs (mostly incendiary from the bomber forces, and a sudden long-range artillery attack against towns within range [this meant towns on the coast of Kent]. It will continue with persistent harassing fire by night on London.

'When weather conditions make enemy air activity impossible, firing can also take place by day. This harassing fire, mingled with bombardments of varying length and intensity, will be calculated so that the supply of ammunition is always related to our capacity for production and transport. In addition, six hundred of these weapons will be regarded as a reserve of the High Command of the Armed Forces [the Oberkommando der Wehrmacht], to be fired only with its approval …'

Thus it was, that on the night of 12/13 June 1944, Hitler's long-awaited V weapons campaign began.

The Royal Observer Corps

It was the ever vigilant members of the Royal Observer Corps who sighted the first of the V1 flying bombs to be fired at the UK that night of 12/13 June 1944, as historian Bob Ogley recalls: 'Local farmer Edwin Woods was on duty on the night of June 12-13 at Observer Post Mike 3, high on the Kent Downs at Lyminge.

Just after 4 am he received a message from Maidstone ROC Centre telling him there was something happening near Boulogne. Mr Wood, through his binoculars, saw a "fighter on fire" but it was just outside his sector. He gave a reading to Maidstone and handed over to his colleagues at Observer post Mike 2 at Dymchurch.'[1]

Mike 2, located at the top of a Martello tower on the seafront at Dymchurch, was manned by Mr E.E. Woodland and Mr A.M. Wraight. 'At 4.08 am they spotted the approach of an object spurting red flames from its rear end and making a noise like "a Model-T-Ford going up a hill". The first flying bomb to be released against England was rattling towards them and the two spotters on top of the tower instinctively knew that the new Battle of Britain had commenced.'

It was the moment that they had been anticipating for months. For the first time the code-word for the new weapon was sounded in alarm – 'Diver, Diver'.

'The men followed the strange object in the sky with their binoculars. When it had approached to within five miles of Mike 2, Mr Woodland seized the telephone and passed the warning to Maidstone ROC Centre. "Mike 2, Diver, Diver, Diver – on four, north-west one-o-one."'

The atmosphere in the underground bunker at ADGD's HQ at Bentley Priory was relaxed that early morning. Suddenly, one of the WAAF tellers sat up as if given an electric shock. She hesitated for a second, as though disbelieving what she had heard in her headphones. Then she called 'Diver, Diver' and the whole Operations Room was galvanised into a frenzy of activity. 'A dozen hands reached for telephones, the main table plotters suddenly forgot their fatigue and the controller watched in amazement as an extraordinary track progressed at great speed across the table towards London.'[2]

The missile continued on it course over the North Downs. Then, at about 04.18 hours, 'the air log propeller on the front of the … V1 … reached its pre-set value. The propeller was linked to a gearing system which counted the miles flown since the missile's launch. At that moment, two igniters were fired which locked the rudder and elevators of the V1 into position and additionally drove two sets of spoilers down from the tail. The deployment of the spoilers ▶

LEFT *A V1 flying bomb pictured on its ramp – its destination, during the summer of 1944, being London or the South East of England. This surviving ramp, the V1 is a replica, can be seen in woodland at Val Ygot near the town of Ardouval, which is, in turn, some fifteen miles south of Dieppe. This launch site was officially known to the Germans as Feuerstellung (or firing point) 685.* (HISTORIC MILITARY PRESS)

disrupted the smooth airflow over the elevators and immediately pitched the missile forward into a steep dive. This sudden change of direction caused a negative G force, which starved the pulse jet of fuel, and the throbbing of the engine suddenly stopped.'[3] In the moments of silence that followed, the bomb dived to the ground, impacting with a loud explosion at Swanscombe, near Gravesend.

Arthur Geering was the head of the Royal Observer Corps at Dymchurch, Kent, and was at his home, which faced out across the Romney Marshes towards the Kent coast, when his team at Mike 2 experienced the arrival of that first V1. 'It was just after four o'clock on the morning of 13 June when my wife suddenly woke me up,' he recalled. 'She said she could hear an aircraft outside making an odd noise. I got out of bed straightaway and went to the window. I could see this aircraft in the half-light and immediately thought, "Cor – he's got an engine on fire," thinking that what I could see was an ordinary plane. I decided to ring my post, Mike Two, at Dymchurch.

'Another post at Folkestone, D Two, apparently also thought there was a crippled plane coming in, and the ROC Centre at Maidstone asked my post if they could see it. Our two chaps on duty, Archie Wright [sic] and Ernie Woodland, had a wonderful pair of American naval binoculars, and as soon as Archie got them trained on the aircraft, he immediately put out the code word "Diver"!

'At the Centre, one of the girls said to her Supervisor, Mike Two says they've got a "Diver" and he said, "For Christ's sake, push it through, then." She did, but Headquarters didn't believe it to start with. They said that if a flying bomb had been launched from France, they would have known about it.

'Well, they soon knew about a few minutes later, when the first one fell near Gravesend. I saw a copy of the report to the Ministry of Home Security which said that it fell on a field growing young greens and lettuces just north of the A2 Rochester-Dartford road. They said it made a crater about twenty feet wide which looked like a saucer, and

destroyed all the crops for about eighty yards all around. There was also a house nearby that was damaged by the blast, but no one inside was injured.'[4]

A shattering explosion

Cyril Oakley was living in Gravesend that first night of the V1 campaign: 'When the sirens in North Kent made their familiar wailing noise in the early hours of June 13, 1944, I was already starved of sleep but somehow made the effort to put on my dressing gown and slippers and rush downstairs and into the garden.

'Overhead, a plane was in trouble, flames were shooting from the rear; it was obviously an enemy bomber which had fallen victim to our defences. I watched it plunge to earth and there was a shattering explosion as it hit the ground somewhere near Swanscombe.'

R.A. Barham was asleep with his family in Ashford: 'At around 4.30 am on June 13, 1944 our family was awakened by a strange menacing sound, once heard never forgotten, but difficult to describe – a sort of stuttering, rattling, deep-throated growl. A plume of fire stretched low across the sky and I told my somewhat disbelieving parents that it was probably a pilotless plane.'[5]

Before there had been time to take stock of the situation at Gravesend, another 'Diver' track had appeared, turned westward, and exploded just north of Cuckfield in Sussex. Two more quickly followed, with one dropping in Bethnal Green and the other close to Sevenoaks in Kent. In fact, a total of ten V1s were launched that night, but five crashed shortly after launching, and a sixth went missing, presumably falling into the Channel.

Alfred Mason was at home when he experienced the effects of the Bethnal Green flying bomb: 'I was in bed and I heard the sirens going in the early hours. But I was one of those cheeky ones and I couldn't be bothered to get out of bed. It was a funny sound and at first I thought it was an airplane. Then it went quiet and the next thing I knew my bedroom walls blew in. I was buried under the rubble for hours before they finally got to me.'[6]

The novelist and short story writer H.E Bates, wrote of his first experience of the first V1s: 'Soon after D-Day, I was at home on leave for two or three days when I woke in the middle of the night to a great and hideous noise and the sight of what was clearly a burning aircraft flying low over the roof of the house. I had never seen a burning aircraft so low at night … I was greatly mystified and, with four young children in the house, not a little frightened.'

The first victims

It was the Bethnal Green bomb which caused the first V1 casualties in the UK. 'The warhead, containing some 850 kilograms of high explosive, detonated in a blinding flash,' wrote former bomb disposal officer Ian Jones MBE. 'After years of pioneering engineering, technical development and testing, the familiar consequence of all the effort was, not surprisingly, the death of innocents. Six people died in the explosion, including Mrs Ellen Woodcraft and her eight-month-old baby Tom; thirty others were seriously injured and a further 200 made homeless.'[7]

Unsurprisingly, the explosion of the first V1 on the British capital generated an immediate response among the authorities, as Ian Jones went on to note: 'At Grove Road, a Royal Engineer Bomb Disposal Officer arrived at the scene to survey the wreckage and institute a search for fragments. As the day progressed his arrival was followed by more, and more senior officials from various organisations.

'By mid-day, in official circles, there was a feeling of relief. The fact was the Germans had launched a total of ten flying bombs that morning with the Tower of London as the central aiming point. Of these, half had crashed on

RIGHT Two members of the Royal Observer Corps – E.E. Woodland, seen here on the left, and A.M. Wraight, on the right – pictured at their post at Dymchurch. When not on duty, they were a greengrocer and builder respectively. Mounted in front of them is an Observer Instrument Mk.2a. When the anti-aircraft guns were moved to the coastal strip, eight were positioned behind the Martello Tower at Dymchurch and at the height of the battle the noise was so intense that the observers had difficulty in making themselves heard.

take-off, one simply disappeared, probably into the Channel, and three exploded in southern England. Only one had reached its intended target. Officials at the site over-estimated the size of the warhead at between 1,200 and 2,000 kilograms of high explosive; but even then, this was significantly less than the ten tons some had feared … General Sir Fredrick Pile noted that, amongst the wreckage at the point of impact, a fuze from a heavy anti-aircraft shell was found. This raised the possibility that his command may have, in fact, shot down the first V1. The fuze could of course have been a relic from a previous raid and the truth will never be known …

'It had previously been arranged with the Ministry of Information that no details of the attack would be

> *"After years of pioneering engineering, technical development and testing, the familiar consequence of all the effort was, not surprisingly, the death of innocents."*

published and there would be no public statement on the new enemy missile. The reason was not so much to deny information to the population of London, but to prevent the Germans gaining knowledge of where the missiles were landing and so enable them to adjust their aim. The result was that the Press was informed that a raider had been shot down and crashed in east London.

'Unfortunately, *The Times*, the following day, reported that the plane had fallen on a railway line in the East End. The Germans had only lost one aircraft over the United Kingdom that night, but this was not operating over London and crashed in Essex, so despite the secrecy, it was obvious that at least one of their missiles had struck close to the intended target. ▶

BELOW A V1 flying bomb is prepared for launching on its ramp – destination London or the South East of England.
(HISTORIC MILITARY PRESS)

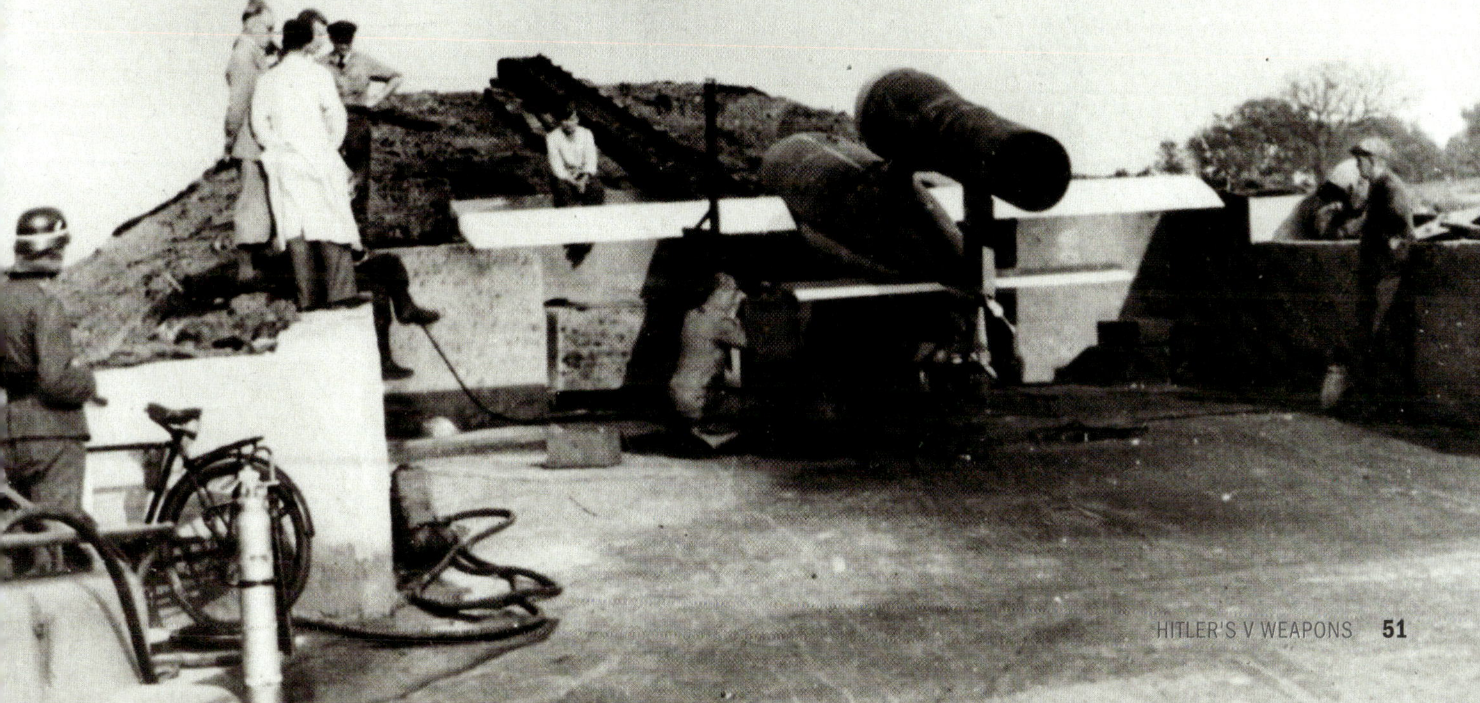

RIGHT AND INSET *The Blue Plaque seen on this railway bridge in Grove Road, Bethnal Green, part of the London Borough of Tower Hamlets, was unveiled in 1988. It marks the spot where the first V1 to fall on London exploded on 13 June 1944. The blast seriously damaged houses in Antill Road, Burnside Street and Bellraven Street, and destroyed the railway line from Liverpool Street to Stratford. Remarkably, railway traffic was restored within forty hours on a temporary bridge that served until 1948.* (COURTESY OF ROBERT MITCHELL)

RIGHT *Another surviving V1 launch ramp in northern France, this time at Feuerstellung 623 which was located near the village of Morbecque in the Pas de Calais – the metal launch rail would have been positioned inside the two walls seen here. The centre of London is 124.8 miles away on a bearing of 297 degrees. Though Feuerstellung 623 was one of the initial ninety-six launch sites built by the Germans in 1943, subsequent attacks by the Allied air forces meant that it was never used operationally in the summer of 1944.* (HISTORIC MILITARY PRESS)

Nevertheless, at the end of the first day, there was considerable optimism amongst some of the senior military and scientific community that the long awaited assault by pilotless aircraft was nowhere near as devastating as had been predicted.'[8]

Indeed, the next day Professor R.V. Jones attended a meeting at the Cabinet Office with Lord Cherwell, Winston Churchill's scientific advisor. Cherwell, Jones recalled, 'was tending to chuckle at the insignificance of the German effort and [he] said, "The mountain hath groaned and given forth a mouse!"'. Jones was sceptical: 'I told him that the night's effort had in my opinion been an organizational hiccup and that within a few days we should see a major bombardment.'[9]

It was only a matter of hours before R.V. Jones' prophetic warning came true. 'Beginning at 22.30 on 15th June, Wachtel [Colonel Max Wachtel, officer in charge of the firing unit] launched more than 200 flying bombs,' he later recounted, 'of which 144 crossed our coasts and 73 reached Greater London. 33 bombs were brought down by the defences but eleven of these came down in the built-up area of Greater London.'[10]

The next day, the 16th, the British public was officially told about the new weapons when Herbert Morrison, the Home Secretary, revealed all to the House of Commons: 'It has been known for some time that the enemy was making preparations for the use of pilotless aircraft against this country,

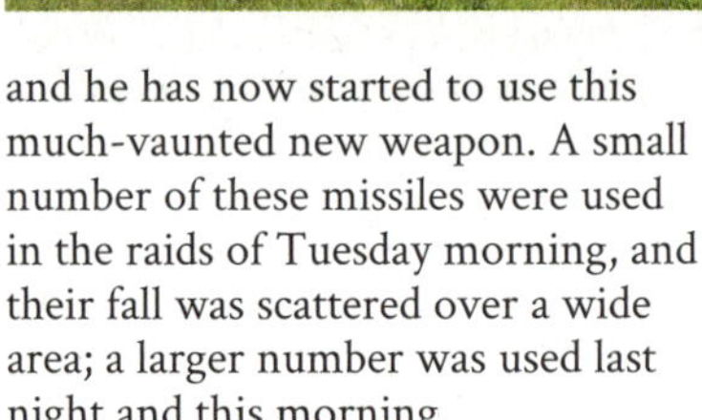

and he has now started to use this much-vaunted new weapon. A small number of these missiles were used in the raids of Tuesday morning, and their fall was scattered over a wide area; a larger number was used last night and this morning.

'On the first occasion, they caused a few casualties, but the attack was light, and the damage, on the whole, was inconsiderable. Last night's attack was more serious, and I have not as yet full particulars of the casualties and damage, nor of the numbers of pilotless aircraft destroyed before they could explode. The enemy's preparations have not, of course, passed unnoticed, and counter-measures have already been, and will continue to be, applied with full vigour. It is, however, probable that the attacks will continue and that, subject to experience, the usual siren warning will be given for such attacks.'[11]

Mr Morrison was, of course entirely correct. The attacks were certainly to continue. ●

NOTES

1 Bob Ogley, *Doodlebugs and Rockets* (Froglets Publications, Brasted Chart, 1992), p.28.

2 Derek Wood, *Attack Warning Red, The Royal Observer Corps and the Defence of Britain 1925 to 1992* (Carmichael & Sweet, Portsmouth, 1992), p.7.

3 Ian Jones MBE, *London – Bombed, Blitzed and Blown Up: The British Capital Under Attack Since 1867* (Frontline Books, Barnsley, 2016), p.263.

4 Quoted in Peter Haining, *The Flying Bomb War* (Robson Books, London, 2002), pp.38-9.

5 Bob Ogley, p.34.

6 Peter Haining, p.40.

7 Ian Jones MBE, pp.263-4.

8 ibid, pp.264-5.

9 R.V. Jones, *Most Secret War* (Hamish Hamilton, London, 1978), p.418.

10 ibid.

11 House of Common Debates, 16 June 1944 vol 400 cc2301-3.

VISIT OUR ONLINE SHOP

TO VIEW OUR FULL RANGE OF SPECIAL MAGAZINES ABOUT HISTORY OF WAR

Key Shop

shop.keypublishing.com/specials

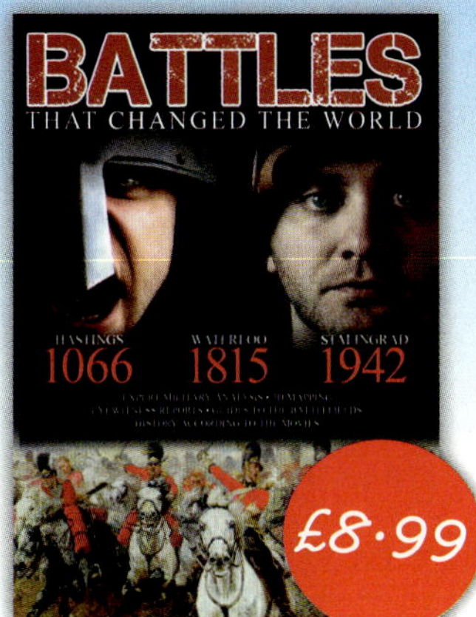

This 100-page special publication sees Robert Kershaw, one of the UK's leading battle historians, take a unique look at three major battles from world history. Originally released in 2012, Battles That Changed The World is a must-read for anyone with an interest in military history.

£8·99

Adolf Hitler capitalised on the seeds of discontent sown by post-World War I 'peace treaties' and waged an embittered campaign of invasion and occupation across mainland Europe.

100 richly illustrated pages – including fascinating images extending over four x four page foldouts.

£5·00

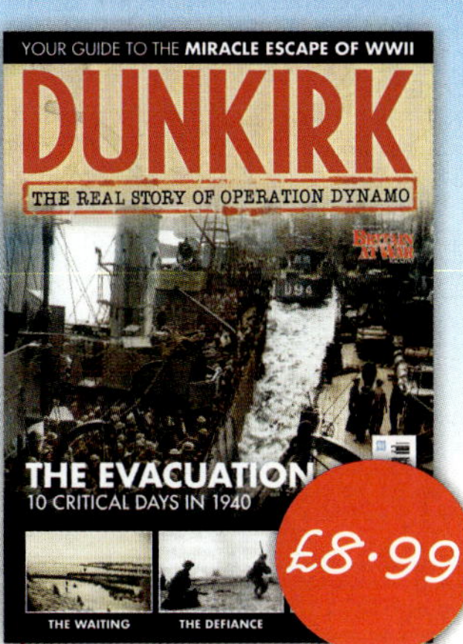

The story of the great evacuation is told, day-by-day, in this 100-page special publication in the words of those soldiers, sailors and airmen who fought and survived those dramatic nine days in the summer of 1940.

£8·99

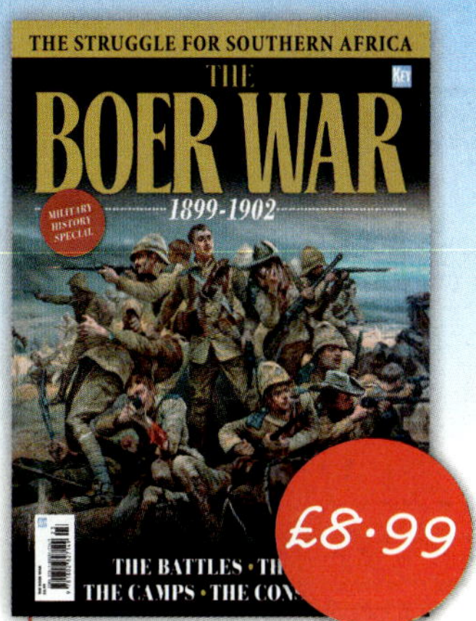

The Second Boer War was Britain's first modern war, delivering many of the challenges that would dominate World War One and beyond.

It was the birthplace of modern guerrilla warfare, concentration camps, blockhouses, and scorched earth tactics.

£8·99

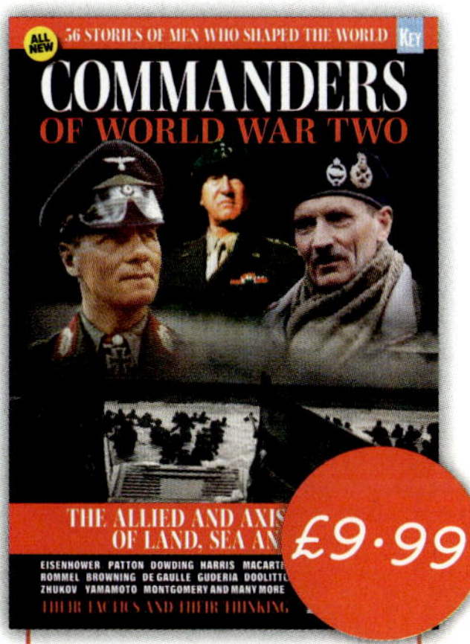

These are the commanders – the decision makers of World War Two. Their military bearing, bravado, skill, and dedication shaped the outcome of the greatest armed conflict in history. Key Publishing presents a frank and comprehensive overview of these intrepid men and their times.

£9·99

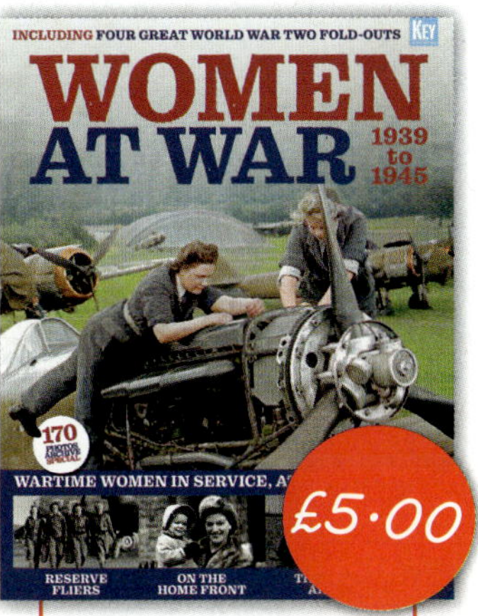

In June 1939, the working population of Britain totalled 19.75 million of which 75% were men. World War Two changed everything, and when the men went to war, the ladies kept industry and agriculture running. They poured into the military too and, by June 1945, 437,000 women were enrolled in the auxiliary services.

£5·00

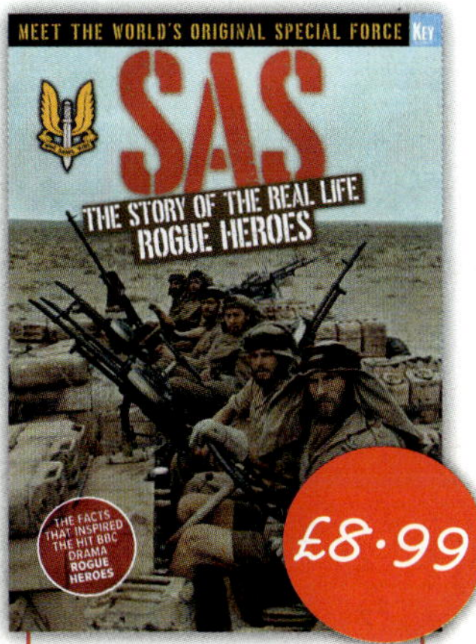

This special publication has been re-released to celebrate the new BBC drama SAS: Rogue Heroes. It looks back to World War Two and its immediate aftermath to recall the men, the missions and the legends of the force that helped turn the tide against the Axis. Written and researched by renowned special forces expert, Gavin Mortimer.

£8·99

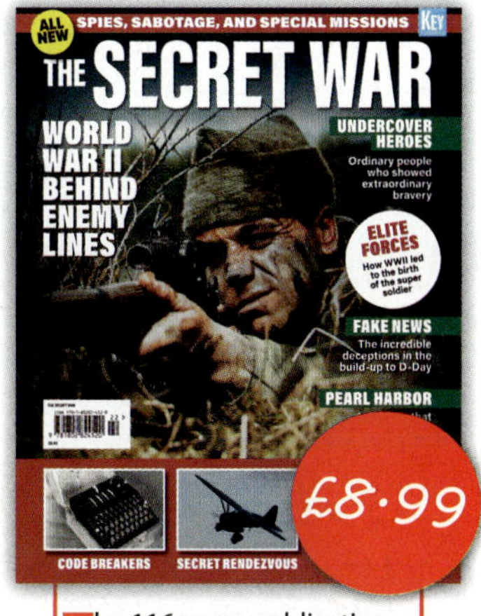

The 116-page publication investigates the Long Range Desert Group, the Jedburghs, and more. We venture behind the veil of secrecy into the world of espionage, examining the Special Operations Executive, the OSS and Abwehr, and their covert operatives – spies – who risked their lives for morsels of intelligence to turn the course of history.

£8·99

FREE P&P* when you order online at...

shop.keypublishing.com/specials

Call +44 (0)1780 480404 *(Monday to Friday 9am-5.30pm GMT)*

Also available from **W.H Smith** and all leading newsagents. Or download from **Pocketmags.com** or your native app store - search *Aviation Specials*

SUBSCRIBERS don't forget to use your **£2 OFF DISCOUNT CODE!**

Free 2nd class P&P on all UK & BFPO orders. Overseas charges apply.

Downing the Doodlebugs

WHEN THE VI CAMPAIGN BEGAN, THE GERMAN MINISTER OF PROPAGANDA, JOSEPH GOEBBELS, CLAIMED THERE WAS NO DEFENCE AGAINST THESE NEW WEAPONS. ALONGSIDE THE OTHER ARMED FORCES DEPLOYED AGAINST THE THREAT, THE RAF WAS DETERMINED TO PROVE OTHERWISE.

RIGHT *A group photograph of 350 (Belgian) Squadron personnel at RAF Hawkinge during 1944. Paul Leva is standing far left, row three.* (COURTESY OF THE LATE PAUL LEVA, VIA TONY MOOR)

I t was certainly true that at first it seemed to many that Goebbels was correct and that there might be no defence against the V1s. 'I remember the first night the buzz bombs came over in earnest,' wrote one soldier stationed near Dover. 'The AA guns kept shooting but never scored a kill. In fact, they kept firing so long the guns were almost horizontal to the ground.'

LEFT *Wing Commander Roland 'Bea' Beamont pictured beside a Tempest V, that coded JF-L, of 3 Squadron at RAF Newchurch in June 1944. Beamont became the first V1 ace, though he would eventually claim a total of thirty-one flying bombs, five of which were shared with other pilots.* (P H.T. GREEN COLLECTION, VIA ANDREW THOMAS)

BELOW *Tempest Vs of 486 Squadron being prepared for anti-Diver patrols at RAF Newchurch in late June or early July 1944. Between them, the two aircraft seen here, JN754 (coded SA-A) and JN801 (coded SA-L), accounted for twenty-four V1s. Both fighters were flown by a number of flying bomb aces. For example, Flight Lieutenant Harvey Sweetman downed three whilst at the controls of JN574 and two in JN801.* (COURTESY OF ANDREW THOMAS)

What was quickly appreciated was that unlike piloted aircraft which took evasive action against guns and searchlights, the V1s continued on a straight, and therefore, predictable path. This enabled the gunners to make accurate calculations in their targeting. Even so, the anti-aircraft guns were having little success against the flying bombs. The main problem was, as noted before, that flying at 2,000 to 3,000 feet the V1s were too high for light guns and too low for heavy guns. Added to this was the fact that the spheres of influence of guns and fighters overlapped, and an awkward system of limiting one or the other according to meteorological conditions was worked out. The radar sets, which had been sited in hollows to avoid enemy jamming, were cluttered up with spurious breaks caused by contours of the ground. The balloon barrage was also extended (eventually, there were 1,750 barrage balloons, creating the largest concentration of balloons ever assembled) which meant that many guns had to be re-sited, with resulting difficulties over the radar. All this resulted in the guns achieving a success rate of less than 10 per cent and the majority of V1s were getting through to London. A major re-think was necessary.

The main anti-aircraft gun employed by General Pile's men was the 3.7-inch. These were mainly mobile guns and were incapable of being traversed quickly enough to shoot the fast-moving, low-flying V1s. Those on static bases were able to traverse more rapidly, but to build concrete bases for hundreds of guns would have taken months, by which time London would have suffered severely. A solution was found by the Royal Electrical and Mechanical Engineers who were able to quickly build platforms composed of a lattice work of steel rails and sleepers filled with ballast. Anti-aircraft accuracy immediately began to rise. Still, two-thirds of all the V1s were getting through the fighters and guns to reach London.

A similar lack of initial success was also experienced by the RAF, as the Mosquito pilots of 96 Squadron at RAF West Malling found: 'The robot bombers started to come in strength tonight and continued in a steady stream into the morning. The ack-ack was terrific and fighters couldn't get anywhere near them, though the CO [Wing Commander Edward Crew DFC] went up specifically to find one.'

The problems associated with trying to shoot down the V1s were explained by Wing Commander Roland Beamont: 'On the first day, speed, height, size and best methods of attack were all unknown. In the event, the attack came gradually at below 2,000 feet and at speeds between 340 and 370 mph IAS; and with a three-foot cross-section fuselage and eight-inch thick wing they proved extremely small targets to hit from the stern quarter which, by virtue of their high speed, was the segment in which the vast majority of fighter attacks ended up. Then there was the question of firing range and how close to go in, relative to the chances of blowing yourself up when the warhead exploded.'[1]

As might be expected, the competition between pilots to be the first to shoot down a V1 by day was intense. That honour went to Flight Sergeant Maurice Rose in a Hawker Tempest of 3 Squadron based at RAF Newchurch near Dungeness in Kent. The date was 16 June 1944, and Rose was one of two pilots who took off ▶

at 07.20 hours. Victory came thirty minutes later. 'The Doodlebug was coming straight out of the sun at my aircraft,' Rose recalled in a newspaper interview. 'Even in the glare I could still see the flame from its motor and the noise of the engine sounded like a motorcycle on the blink.

'I am used to facing Hun fighter pilots who always try to come out of the sun at you – but they twist and turn to make it difficult for you to get a clean shot. But this new Nazi terror weapon didn't deviate an inch as it came straight on towards me. The whole situation seemed crazy, almost unreal. But there was no time to think. I had set my sights and went into action. I was about to do something no fighter pilot had ever

done before. Go into battle against a robot enemy.'[2]

The V1 burst into flames before crashing to the ground near Maidstone. Far from savouring the moment, Rose had other issues to contend with, for no sooner had he despatched the flying bomb then his Tempest was fired on, and hit, by a US Army anti-aircraft unit. Despite a hole in the wing that later necessitated a complete wing change, Rose managed to land back at Newchurch.[3]

In his newspaper interview, Rose then talked about further sorties against the V1s: 'The first thing you hear is the sound like an angry bee and then a tiny speck of light appears over the horizon growing bigger every second. The buzz and the light soon become synchronised into what appears to be a meteor with a flaming orange-red tail.

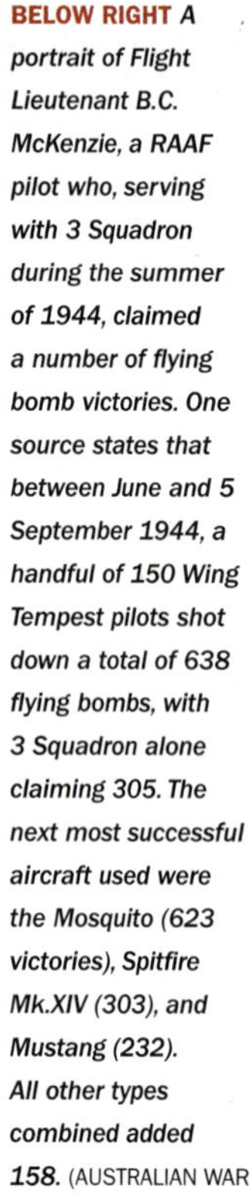

'Sometimes near the coast, ack-ack guns will open up below you and you can see red and white tracer shots streaming up towards the robot. If they hit the intruder all well and good, but if they don't then it becomes your turn to go in. Of course, it has become part of our tactics to attack the robots before they reach the coast so we don't run the risk of being hit by the ack-ack fire ourselves!

'As you close up on the robot, it looks rather like a large flame with wings sticking out on either side. Because it is so small, the flying bomb is not easy to hit, but it is still vulnerable. If your bullets strike home on the jet unit, the whole thing catches fire and it goes down with a crash. If you hit the explosives it is carrying, the robot blows up.

'When we started attacking these machines we trod warily, shooting

from long range, but as we have got experienced at this new form of attack, we have found we can close in, sometimes to 100 yards. If you are close when the bomb goes up you sometimes fly through the debris, and some of our Tempests have come back with their paint scorched. Some have even been turned on their backs by the force of the explosion, but the pilot feels no effect except an upward jolt.

'Often it is not necessary to hit your target cleanly. A few bullets sometimes upset the gyro (automatic pilot) and the robot crashes down into the sea. One of our chaps has also discovered that by using his slipstream it is possible to force the Doodlebugs into a spin.'[4]

A balancing act

As well as bringing the flying bombs down by spinning them in the slipstream of the fast fighters, another

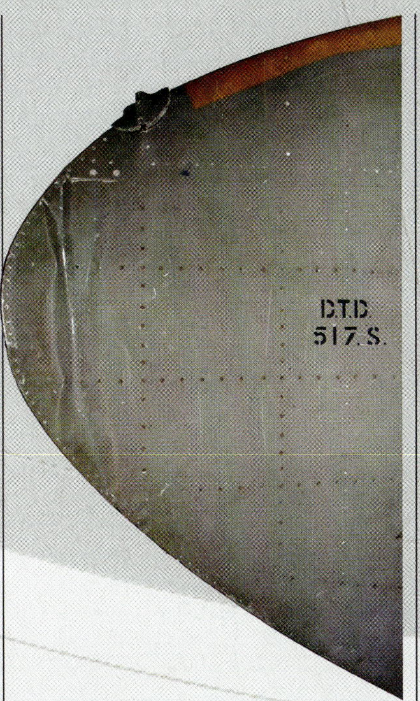

method was attempted by Paul 'Pino' Leva of 350 (Belgian) Squadron based at RAF Hawkinge. It was there, on Sunday, 20 August 1944, along with other pilots of 'B' Flight, Leva was listening to a briefing from an Intelligence Officer who detailed the tactics employed so far to bring down the flying bombs. The squadron had recently been equipped with the Spitfire Mk.XIVe, but even with this advanced fighter, the V1s were still difficult, if not impossible, to catch up with from behind. The only way the pilotless aircraft could be attacked, the Intelligence Officer explained, was by a diving attack, in which the speed gained in the dive would enable the pilot to close, briefly, to within firing range.

> *"...directed by the controller, I duly spotted the ugly little brute with the glowing tail below me. I banked to enter a steep dive, gathering speed and getting nearer and nearer to my target."*

The Intelligence Officer also said, based no doubt upon the kind of experiences referred to by the pilots of 3 Squadron, that if the V1's lateral stability was disturbed by an outside element (such as a slipstream) the bomb could not re-stabilise itself and would spin to the ground. The Intelligence Officer also speculated that if a pilot was able to put a wing under one of the flying bombs and nudge it with sufficient force, there was every chance that the V1's gyro would be unbalanced, and it would crash out of the sky.

Leva's 'B' Flight took off that afternoon at 14.50 hours to go 'Doodlebug hunting'. Leva was at the controls of RM701, coded MN-O. 'I

ABOVE RIGHT
The late Paul Leva displays the wing tip of the Spitfire Mk.XIVe, RM701 coded MN-O, in which he destroyed a V1 by 'tipping' it over. (COURTESY OF THE LATE PAUL LEVA, VIA TONY MOOR)

ABOVE LEFT *The paintwork on the starboard wing tip of RM701 remains in good condition.* (COURTESY OF TONY MOOR)

MIDDLE LEFT *The first interception of a V1 was made by Flight Lieutenant John Musgrave, seen here on the left, in a 605 Squadron Mosquito VI on the night of 15/16 June 1944. To Musgrave's left is his navigator, Sergeant F.W. Samwell. The pair eventually claimed a total of twelve flying bombs.* (605 SQUADRON/I. PIPER, VIA ANDREW THOMAS)

… climbed as quickly as possible to a nice comfortable altitude from where, in principle, I would be able to dive on any bomb passing underneath me,' Leva later recounted to the author and historian Tony Moor.

'Soon after, the familiar voice of the controller came on, telling me that a flying-bomb had been spotted on the radar and he gave me its position and its heading. This did not yet mean that I would have a chance to attack it. Indeed, since the middle of July the plan against the "buzz-bomb" comprised of four defence belts. These were a fighter zone from mid-Channel to the coast, an AA gun belt on the coast itself, then the inner Fighter Patrol Zone, which extended from the gun belt to the balloon barrage south-east of London which formed the fourth zone. This meant that only if the bomb was missed by the fighters over the channel and also by the guns on the coast would I have the opportunity to chase it.

'As it was, the bomb went unscathed through the two first defence lines and, directed by the controller, I duly spotted the ugly little brute with the glowing tail below me. I banked to enter a steep dive, gathering speed and getting nearer and nearer to my target. Alas, though, I was not near enough. Soon, with my speed dropping after levelling off, I could see that the distance separating us did not diminish further and even began to increase.'

Leva was over the Tonbridge area by this time, getting ever closer to the London barrage balloon belt. 'Utterly disappointed, I nevertheless opened fire, aiming high to compensate ▶

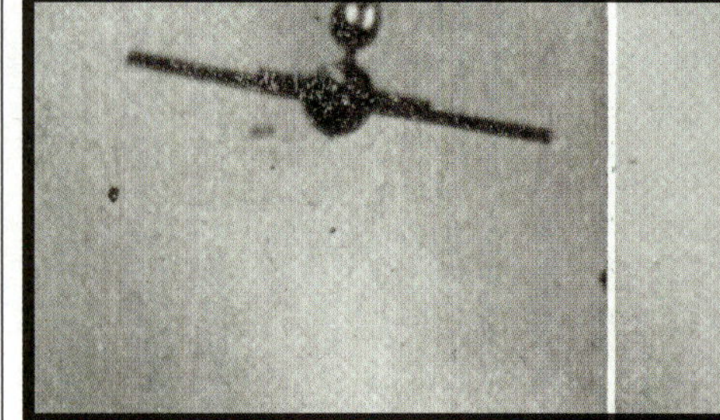

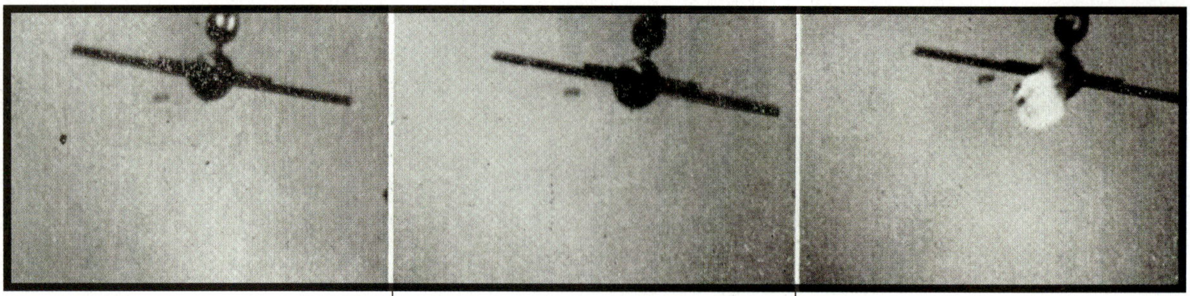

BELOW *All four of these 315 Squadron pilots found success against V1s in 1944. They are, from left to right on the wing, Warrant Officer Tadeusz Slon (one and two shared), Flight Lieutenant Michal Cwynar (two and four shared), and Flight Lieutenant Jerzy Schmidt (two and two shared). In the foreground is Flight Sergeant Tadeusz Jankowki, 315 Squadron's leading V1 ace, with four and six shared destroyed.* (COURTESY OF ANDREW THOMAS)

for the distance and I had the happy surprise to see some impacts and bits flying off the wings. I fired burst after burst, damaging the bomb still more. Although no vital part was hit, its speed diminished, and it entered into a shallow dive.

'My hopes were soaring again. I was now approaching my target, so fast that I had to throttle back. Ready for the kill, I positioned myself at what I estimated was the right distance. I depressed the trigger, but instead of the staccato of firing bullets I heard only the whistling sound of escaping compressed air.

'The voice of the controller came again: "Any luck?"

'"No," I said forlornly. "I damaged it, but I have no ammunition left. It's very slow and losing height. I am practically flying formation with it."

'"Tough luck," said the controller. "Time to turn back now – you are getting very near the balloon barrage". It was then that suddenly, spurred no doubt by my frustration, I remembered the briefing of the intelligence officer, who earlier had spoken of sending V1s out of control by tipping up one wing.

'"Wait," I said. "I think I can try something'. Adjusting the throttle, I eased myself forward until I came abreast of the bomb. What a sight it was at close range! The wings were so ragged with the impact of the bullets that I wondered how it could still fly almost straight and level.

'Positioning myself slightly underneath, I placed my starboard wing tip under the port wing of the bomb. I came up slowly, made contact with it as softly as I could, and then moved the stick violently back and to the left. This made me enter a steep climbing turn and I lost sight of the bomb. I continued turning fast through 360 degrees, then I saw it well below me, going down steeply, hitting the ground and exploding with a blinding flash.'

Though there is also a claim made by a Polish pilot of 316 (City of Warsaw) Squadron to have been the first to bring a V1 down by tipping it over, for his feat Leva was given his damaged wing tip as a souvenir. It is said that some fighter pilots became so proficient at dealing with the V1s in this manner, that they were able to actually turn the flying bombs around so that they headed back towards their bases in the Pas-de-Calais.[5]

The fight at night

As also discussed earlier, the next step taken by General Pile to improve the success rate of his guns was to move the defensive belt from around London down to the south coast. Almost immediately, the success rate against the V1s began to improve. New American

radar sets and predictors were also received, greatly improving accuracy. This was especially the case at night or in bad weather. The V1s, of course, could fly in any weather conditions, but the guns and the RAF pilots relied on good weather to see their targets. The new American equipment helped the gunners considerably during those times of limited visibility. At the same time the problem of exploding the shells at the correct height was solved by the introduction of the proximity fuze. The US also supplied twenty anti-aircraft batteries equipped with 90mm heavy guns. The total of heavy guns in the belt rose to nearly 600.

Interspersed with more normal equipment along the belt were anti-aircraft tanks, experimental versions of various guns, Petroleum Warfare Department 9-inch mortars, 2-inch Naval rockets and others. More was learnt about the potentialities of anti-aircraft work in eighty days, Pile claimed, than had been learned in the previous thirty years. In addition, one Searchlight Regiment was converted to a rocket role and manned four twin Rocket Batteries, 512 barrels in all.

The original inland searchlight belt did not move to the coast with the guns and it was only at

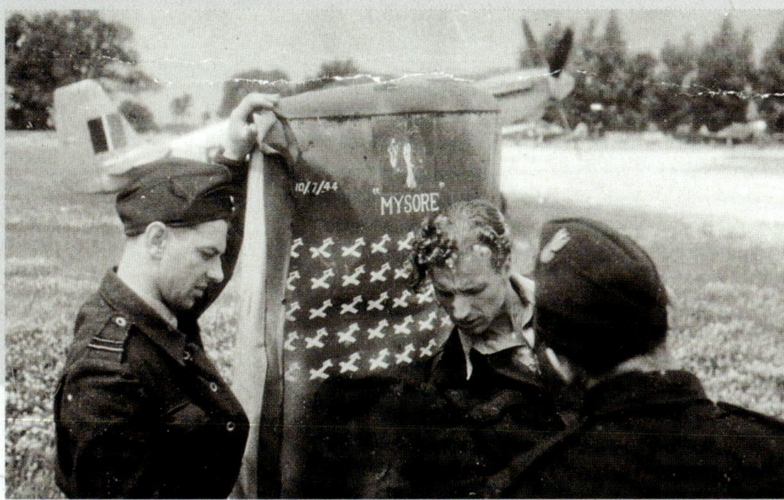

LEFT *The recovered wing of a V1 brought down on 10 July 1944, was put into service as a scoreboard by the pilots of the Brenzett-based 129 (Mysore) Squadron.* (W. MATUSIAK, VIA ANDREW THOMAS)

BELOW LEFT *On 1 July 1944, Flying Officer G.P. Armstrong of 165 Squadron intercepted a V1 which blew up near his aircraft. The evidence of this combat can clearly be seen in this picture of Armstrong posing for the camera by Spitfire IX MJ221, coded SK-J, after landing.* (CHARLES YOUNG, VIA ANDREW THOMAS)

RIGHT *Destroying more than sixty V1s, Flight Lieutenant Joe Berry, who was promoted Squadron Leader in August 1944 and took command of 501 Squadron, was the most successful pilot in the battle against the flying bombs. Initially flying Tempest Vs with the Fighter Interception Unit, Berry claimed his first V1s during the afternoon of 28 June.* (501 SQUADRON ASSOCIATION, VIA ANDREW THOMAS)

this stage that it began to give full value. There were now two fighter areas, one out to sea and one behind the gun belt. With the latter the searchlights co-operated at night. Although the flame from the propulsion unit of the flying bomb made it self-illuminating at night, fighters were not usually able to judge its distance or course without the assistance of a searchlight intersection, especially while making a fast dive and turn towards it. Owing to the low flying height of the bomb a rapid traverse was required and this called for skilful operation, especially since it was essential not to dazzle the fighter, which, at such low heights and high speeds, would then have been in imminent danger of crashing. Of the targets which penetrated

> *"...it was decided by the RAF top brass to see if some of the night-fighter pilots could convert to flying the Tempest more easily than the day fighter pilots could convert to all-weather night flying..."*

the coastal belt at night, searchlights assisted fighters in the destruction of 142, or something over 30 per cent.

The pilot credited with shooting down the first V1 at night was Flight Lieutenant John Musgrave flying a Mosquito of 605 Squadron. The most successful of the night fighters, as it transpired, was also from the same squadron – No.3 – as Maurice Rose, Squadron Leader Joseph Berry who, by the end of August 1944 had claimed sixty V1s, all at night. His largest haul was in shooting down seven of the flying bombs in a single night, 23 July.

Berry spoke of his experiences in a BBC radio broadcast on 30 August: 'As many of you will probably know, the first of these flying bombs, or "doodlebugs" as they are popularly

called, were first fired at us by the Germans during the daytime. Our fighter pilots could see them coming and were able to pick a lot of them off in the air.

'Soon the Germans started to send them over at night when the only thing that was visible were the flames coming from their jet engines. To start with, some of our day fighter pilots were sent to try to intercept these robots. Normally these pilots in their Tempests and Spitfires are crack shots, but it soon became apparent that they were not sufficiently at home in the dark clouds of night.

'Because of the urgency of the situation, it was decided by the RAF top brass to see if some of the night-fighter pilots could convert to flying the Tempest more easily than the day fighter pilots could convert to all-weather night flying … It was in July that I was posted as a squadron leader to organise night flying against the doodlebugs. Although my squadron had to put up with a lot of leg-pulling in the officers' mess whenever low clouds or rain prevented us from flying, once we were airborne there were usually rich pickings to be had … But don't get the idea that the doodlebug goes down easily. It will take a lot of punishment and the pilot has to aim at the propulsion unit – that's a long stove-pipe, as we call it, on the tail.

'If your range and aim are dead on, you can see pieces flying off the stove-pipe. The big white flame at the end then goes out, and down goes the bomb. Sometimes it dives straight to earth, but at other times it goes crazy and gives a wizard display of aerobatics before finally crashing.

'Sometimes the bomb explodes in the air, and the flash is so blinding that you cannot see a thing for about ten seconds. You hope to be the right ▶

way up when you are able to see again, because the explosion often throws the fighter about and sometimes even turns it upside down.'[6]

The jet age

By early August 1944 the combined efforts of the Anti-Aircraft Command and the Allied air forces had very much mastered the skills and organisational techniques for dealing with the V1s. The air defence of the UK was then bolstered further with the introduction of a new type of aircraft, one that could travel even faster than the flying bombs – Britain's first jet fighter, the Gloster Meteor.

RIGHT *One of 616 (South Yorkshire) Squadron's Gloster Meteors pictured at RAF Manston in the summer of 1944. This particular aircraft, EE219 coded YQ-D, was flown by Flying Officer McKenzie on the first Meteor operational sortie on 27 July 1944.* (COURTESY OF T.R. ALONBY, VIA ANDREW THOMAS)

RIGHT *A Gloster Meteor Mk.I of 616 Squadron pictured in flight over the Kent countryside between West Hougham and Dover, 10 August 1944.* (COURTESY OF ANDY THOMAS)

BELOW *One of 616 Squadron's Meteors, EE227 coded YQ-Y, scrambles from RAF Manston during August 1944. The squadron flew standing patrols throughout the V1 campaign, with two aircraft airborne at all times when conditions permitted.* (COURTESY OF M. PAYNE, VIA ANDREW THOMAS)

The first squadron to be equipped with the new aircraft was 616 (South Yorkshire) Squadron operating from RAF Manston in Kent, right at the heart of what had become known as 'Doodle-Bug Alley'. Given the squadron's base it was only natural that the unit should immediately be thrown into the defensive fighter line that was put up constantly during that summer to counter the flying bomb threat.

Although 616 Squadron flew its first Meteor-equipped anti-V1 patrol on Thursday, 27 July 1944, it was a little over a week later that the squadron's Meteors scored their first success. All through the preceding week there had been a number of close-calls as 616's Meteors came close to achieving victory several times, but it was on Friday, 4 August 1944 that what has sometimes been called the first successful jet-on-jet encounter occurred.[7]

That morning, a summer haze and poor visibility had prevented any success by the patrolling Meteor pilots. Doubtless, this was doubly frustrating given that the previous day, 3 August, had seen the climax of the V1, or Diver, attacks with an astonishing 316 missiles launched from France – of which 220 reached British soil. Thus, not only was the 'hunting' for the RAF's fighter pilots at its peak but, also, the need to intercept them became ever more pressing.

By afternoon on the 4th, however, the weather situation had improved. As a result, when Flying Officer Thomas Derek 'Dixie' Dean and Flying Officer 'Jock' Rodger were scrambled from Manston during the mid-afternoon there seemed reasonable prospects for an engagement.

The plan of attack

The modus operandi for the Meteor pilots on their anti-Diver patrols was to operate in a pair and loiter above the anticipated approach route for the weapons – but at a higher altitude than the 1,000 to 3,000 feet at which the V1s generally appeared. Once an incoming missile had been spotted against the countryside below, often sighted after guns and other defences in the anti-aircraft belt had provided a clue of where to look, the jet pilots would then get into an attacking position, open up the throttles and go into a dive, trading height for speed. This would often be a speed in excess of 400mph although, in actual fact, the maximum speed of the Meteor I was 415mph; coincidentally, the cruising speed of the V1 was also 415mph. That said, the missiles routinely came in at speeds between 380 and 400mph, but it was preferable, if not essential, for the Meteor pilots to have the advantage of

ABOVE *A stunning shot of EE222 which, coded YQ-G, was flown by Wing Commander Andrew McDowall on 27 July 1944, 616 Squadron's first day on operations whilst flying the Meteor.* (COURTESY OF T.R. ALLONBY, VIA ANDREW THOMAS)

speed in their diving interceptions. Such was the case when Dixie Dean, call sign *Hugo 24*, spotted his quarry. He takes up the story in his Combat Report:

'At 15.45 hours I was "scrambled" (under Kinsley 11 Control) for Anti Diver patrol between Ashford and Robertsbridge. Flying at 4,500 ft at 340mph indicated air speed I saw one Diver four to five miles south east of Tenterden flying at 1,000 feet on a course of 330°, estimated speed of 365mph (16.16 hours). From two and a half miles behind the Diver I dived down from 4,500 feet at 470 mph.

'Closing in to attack I found my four x 20mm guns would not fire owing to a technical trouble now being investigated. I then flew my Meteor alongside the Diver for approximately twenty to thirty seconds. Gradually I manoeuvred my wing tip a few inches under the wing of the Diver, then pulling my aircraft upwards and sharply I turned the Diver over onto its back and sent it diving to earth at approximately four miles south of Tonbridge [*sic*].

'On return to Manston I was informed that the ROC [Royal Observer Corps] had confirmed one

RIGHT *On the night of 16/17 July 1944, 2 Lieutenant Herman Ernst took off from RAF Ford, with Flight Officer Ed Kopsel, at the controls of a Northrop P-61A Black Widow, 42-5547 which was nicknamed Borrowed Time, of the USAAF's 422nd Night Fighter Squadron. They were vectored onto a V1, which they shot down into the Channel. It was both the type's and the unit's first kill of the war.* (H. ERNST/W. THOMPSON, VIA ANDREW THOMAS)

LEFT *Wing Commander Andrew McDowall was the Officer Commanding 616 Squadron at the time of its deployment against the flying bombs in August 1944.* (COURTESY OF ANDY THOMAS)

Diver had crashed at the position given by me. This is the first pilotless aircraft to be destroyed by a jet-propelled aircraft.'

Ready for More

Shortly after Flying Officer Dean's victory, another of 616 Squadron's pilots also achieved success in his Meteor. This time the victor was Flying Officer J.K. 'Jock' Rodger, call sign *Hugo 18*. Once again, the subsequent combat report takes up the story:

'Under "Kingsley 11 Control" I was "scrambled" and vectored to patrol in vicinity of Ashford/Tenterden. Divers were reported to be coming in at 3,000 feet between Tenterden and coast. At 16.40 hours I sighted a Diver near Tenterden flying on a course of 318° at 3,000 feet, estimated speed 340mph.

'I immediately attacked from dead astern and fired a 2 seconds burst at

> *"Gradually I manoeuvred my wing tip a few inches under the wing of the Diver, then pulling my aircraft upwards and sharply I turned the Diver over onto its back and sent it diving to earth."*

range of 300 yards. I observed hits and saw petrol and/or oil streaming out of Diver which continued to fly straight and level. I fired another 2 seconds burst from my 4 cannon still from 300 yards. Both Meteor and Diver were flying at 340mph. The Diver then went down and I saw it explode on ground about 5 miles North West of Tenterden.'

Rodger timed the explosion as having been at 16.55 hours. This was the V1 that fell at Biddenden causing damage to a number of cottages but resulting in no casualties.

Buoyed by these first two successes, the following entry was made in the 616 Squadron's Operations Record Book at the end of 4 August: 'The Squadron, now thrilled at the first two kills, is ready for more.' There would indeed be more V1 'kills' ▶

by the jets of 616 Squadron before the campaign was brought to a close in September 1944 when Allied ground forces overran the ski sites in northern France.

Just as the RAF was increasingly successful in intercepting the V1s so too was the re-adjusted anti-aircraft gun belt. The degree of improvement since the period of the inland belt at the start of the V1 campaign when

the successes were under 10 per cent, is shown in the percentages of flying bombs destroyed in the following successive weeks; these were, in the first phase of the coastal belt, 17 per cent, 24 per cent, 27 per cent, 40 per cent and 55 per cent, and, in the second phase of the coastal belt, 60 per cent and 74 per cent.

Altogether, 4,261 V1s were destroyed by fighters, anti-aircraft fire and barrage balloons, out of a total of 8,025 that were sent against the UK. Many more flying bombs would have reached the UK but for the efforts of Bomber Command and the USAAF which continued to attack the 'ski sites' and suspected assembly and manufacturing buildings, as Operation *Crossbow* continued throughout the summer of 1944. ●

NOTES

1 Quoted in Brian Cull, *Diver! Diver! Diver! RAF and American Fighter Pilots Battle the V-1 Assault over South-East England 1944-45* (Grub Street, London, 2008), p.42.

2 *Empire News*, 20 July 1944.

3 Chris Thomas, *Tempest Squadrons of the RAF* (Osprey, London, 2016), p.16.

4 *Empire News*, 20 July 1944.

5 Peter Haining, *The Flying Bomb War, Contemporary Eyewitness Accounts of the German V-1 and V-2 Raids on Britain* (Robson, London, 2002), p.78.

6 A complete transcript of the BBC broadcast was also published in the *Listener Magazine* in 1944.

7 Whilst the Meteor was a jet-engine aeroplane, the V1 was powered by a ram-jet propulsion unit; the first true jet-on-jet encounter did not occur until the Korean War.

VISIT OUR ONLINE SHOP

Key Shop

TO VIEW OUR FULL RANGE OF **HISTORIC BOOKS**

shop.keypublishing.com/books

NEW

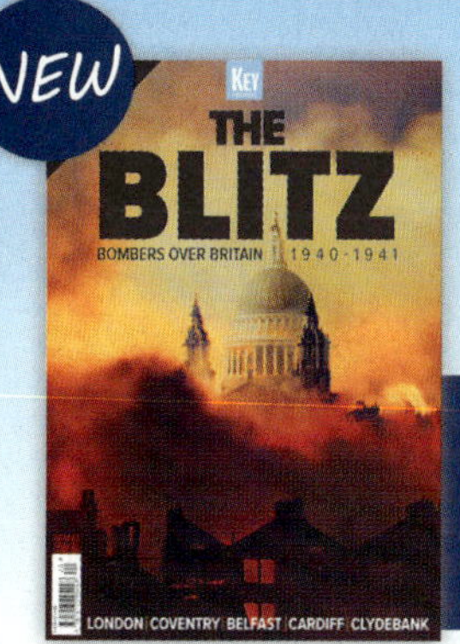

For months 'The Few' had defended Britain against the might of the Luftwaffe. Then, on September 7, 1940 everything changed. The Blitz had begun. With sections examining life in the shelters, Britain's defences, bomb disposal and examining the darker side of the Blitz – looting – this essential book containing more than 190 images looks back to discover what life was really like in late 1940.

ONLY £15·99
SUBSCRIBERS don't forget to use your **£2 OFF DISCOUNT CODE!**

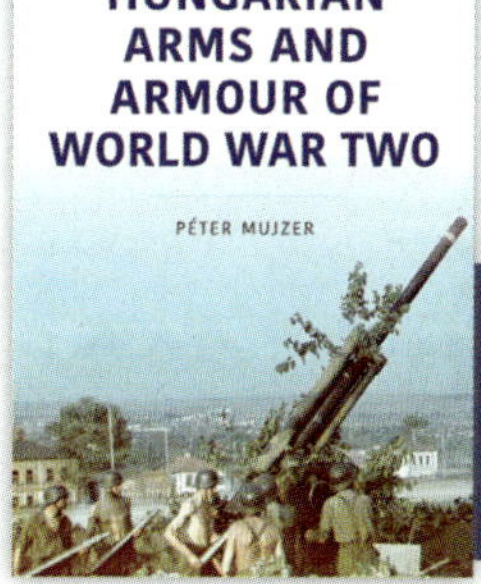

There are over 40 surviving World War Two tanks, self-propelled guns, tank destroyers, tank hunters and tank turrets in the Belgium and Luxembourg Ardennes. Illustrated with over 150 images and containing detailed descriptions of the tanks and where to find them, this book is an invaluable resource for anyone visiting the Ardennes.

ONLY £15·99
SUBSCRIBERS don't forget to use your **£2 OFF DISCOUNT CODE!**

In World War Two, the German army deployed a wide variety of tanks in many different variants and forms of camouflage. These tanks were often lethal to become entangled with and known to be formidable pieces of military engineering. This book features a unique collection of colour illustrations which detail their development, differences in design and modifications that were made during their production run.

ONLY £14·99
SUBSCRIBERS don't forget to use your **£2 OFF DISCOUNT CODE!**

During World War Two, Hungary found itself in opposition to the Allied nations, and although in 1941 the war was remote, in 1944 45 it arrived in Hungary, crushing the kingdom. This book gives a brief history of the Hungarian Army, focusing on the main armament of the land forces: armoured vehicles, artillery pieces, infantry weapons and motor vehicles.

ONLY £15·99
SUBSCRIBERS don't forget to use your **£2 OFF DISCOUNT CODE!**

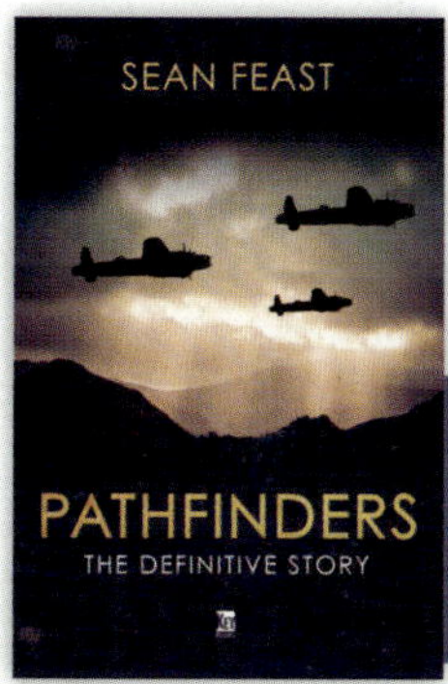

Pathfinders is a new history of Bomber Command's corps d'elite and the men who led the greatest striking force ever known. The story explores the genesis of Pathfinder Force (PFF), from its initial inception and less-than-spectacular start to its development as a precision instrument that gave the razor edge to the RAF bomber offensive.

ONLY £25·00
SUBSCRIBERS don't forget to use your **£2 OFF DISCOUNT CODE!**

This book gives the reader, be they well-versed in Luftwaffe matters or just simply curious to know more, an insight into the main Luftwaffe fighters of World War Two. The book also includes unit, campaign and combat histories so as to give an idea of what it was like to fly or fight in these aircraft between 1939 and 1945.

ONLY £18·99
SUBSCRIBERS don't forget to use your **£2 OFF DISCOUNT CODE!**

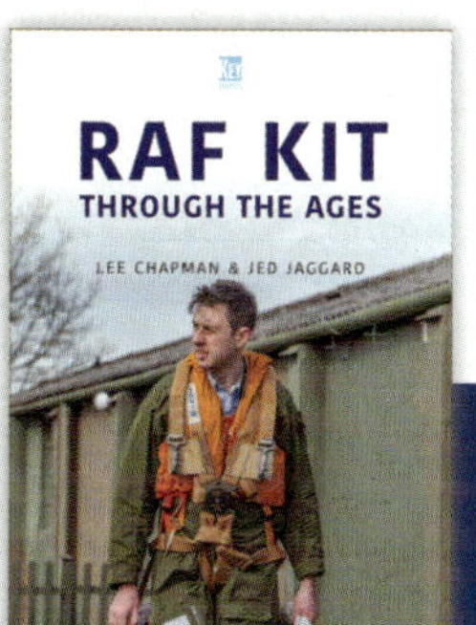

This book studies the history of the RAF's pilot and aircrew kit, exploring how the personal equipment and flying gear issued to service personnel has changed over the last century. This informative new book features more than 100 full colour photographs of original and authentic replica kit as worn by RAF aircrew throughout history.

ONLY £15·99
SUBSCRIBERS don't forget to use your **£2 OFF DISCOUNT CODE!**

This guide book examines the surviving WWII tanks, tank turrets and other armoured fighting vehicles currently on display in Normandy, France, most of which took part in the fighting following the D-Day landings. The background history of each vehicle is explored and location details are given.

ONLY £15·99
SUBSCRIBERS don't forget to use your **£2 OFF DISCOUNT CODE!**

FREE P&P* when you order online at...
shop.keypublishing.com/books

Call +44 (0)1780 480404 *(Monday to Friday 9am-5.30pm GMT)*

Free 2nd class P&P on all UK & BFPO orders. Overseas charges apply.

Listening for Silence

NEVER BEFORE HAD A CIVILIAN POPULATION COME UNDER SUCH A SUSTAINED ATTACK FROM MISSILES SUCH AS HITLER'S V1 FLYING BOMB.

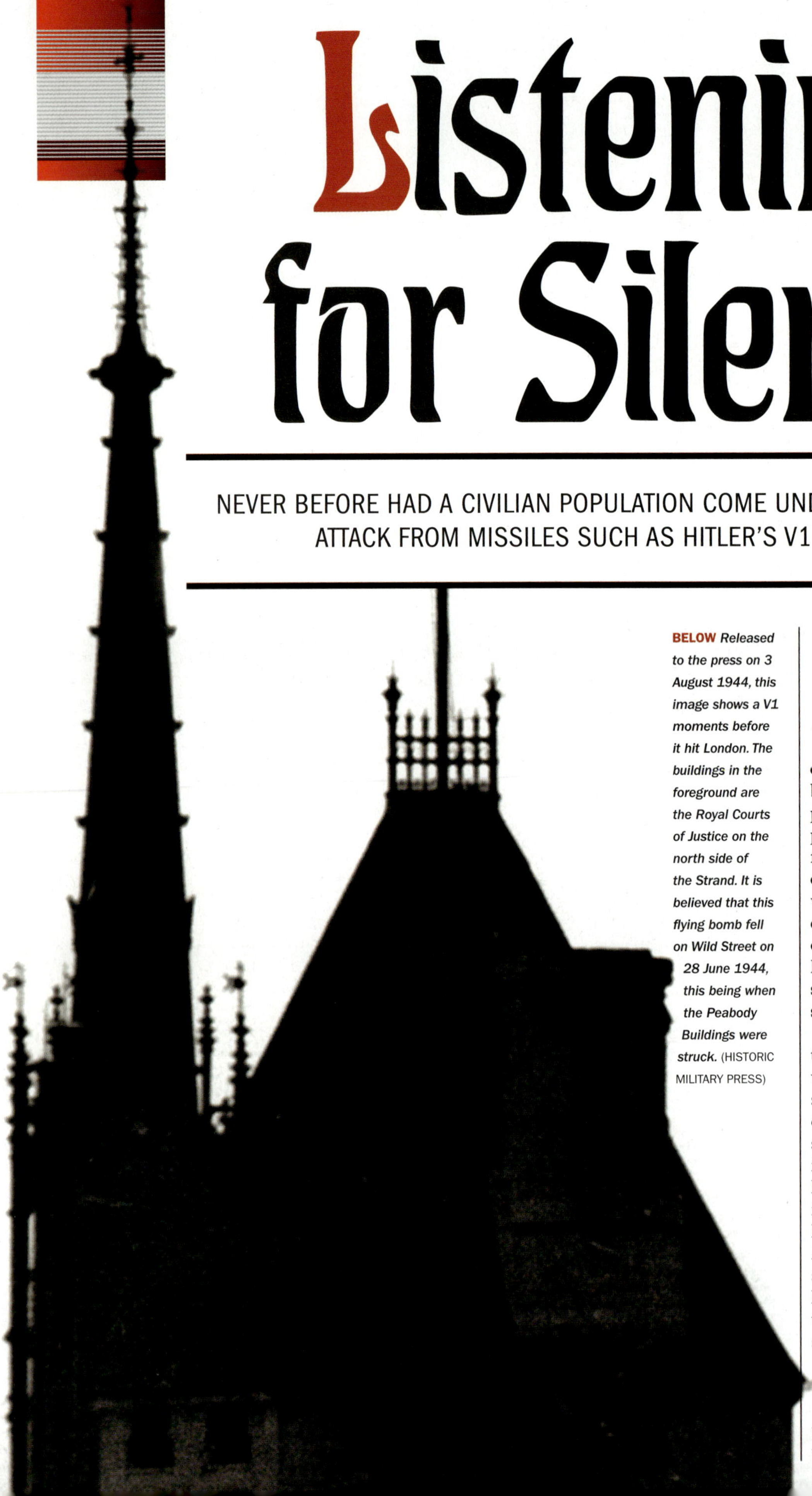

BELOW *Released to the press on 3 August 1944, this image shows a V1 moments before it hit London. The buildings in the foreground are the Royal Courts of Justice on the north side of the Strand. It is believed that this flying bomb fell on Wild Street on 28 June 1944, this being when the Peabody Buildings were struck.* (HISTORIC MILITARY PRESS)

Once officially acknowledged, and as the intensity of the bombardment gathered pace, the flying bomb offensive came as a psychological blow to many, particularly the population of London. This was perhaps unsurprising for in the first fortnight of the attacks the casualty rate in the British capital was as high as in the same period of the Blitz, though the proportion of injuries to deaths was much higher since the V1s as often struck during the day when the streets were crowded.[1]

To those who were able to observe the passage of one of Hitler's new weapons from a position of relative safety, they were often an object of great fascination. As a young schoolboy, Tom Pollitt recalled his first experience of a V1. At the time he had been enjoying a precious few moments with his father. The latter, a Sergeant Major in the Royal Artillery who was based at a heavy anti-aircraft gun site near Dover, was home on leave: 'The siren went, and we all went in the backyard Anderson shelter. We heard what I thought was a low flying bomber, but my Dad knew only too well what it was! He took me to the door and showed me this long flame speeding overhead. It was my first sighting of a V1 flying

bomb, or "Doodlebug" as they were called. It roared over with a sound like half-a-dozen Harleys. My Dad said, "Don't worry about the noise it makes – it's when the engine stops that you should worry!"'[2]

For Joan Millar, a comparable experience saw danger creep a little closer. 'During the spring and summer of 1944,' she remembered, 'I went down to Kent nearly every weekend to visit my aunt and see my dog. I used to take the train to Tonbridge and bike the rest of the way, an uphill journey: my aunt's house was right out in the open countryside near Plaxtol. It was in her garden that she and I first saw a flying bomb. We had heard it as it passed directly overhead and dashed into the garden to find out what it was. It was still making that peculiar "rump, rump" noise and as far as I remember it had a burning red "nose". It looked so odd that we turned to one another and burst out laughing; then came the fearful silence, followed by a crash – fortunately on open ground some way away.'[3]

Barry Cogswell found himself in a similar situation to Joan, though he was even closer to the inevitable outcome. At the time he was living with his parents in Purley. His father, believing that the worst of the Blitz was over, had moved his previously evacuated family back to this part of South London in 1942.

'To us young boys of five or six,' Barry recalls, 'the putt, putt, putt of a doodlebug on a warm drowsy summer day was very exciting … When you are five, there seems no danger. Rather, there is a kind of excitement as we children learned of the latest technologies and war machines … However, the danger was real.

'One morning, for no particular reason that I can remember, my mother and I were standing outside the front door looking over the suburban valley below, a doodlebug flew not 100 yards in front of us. It came from the south, in a shallow dive. In my memory, time slowed for a while as it glided past at a leisurely pace and at eye level. In reality, though, it was probably in sight for only two or three seconds.

'I had time to note the grey paint and yellow, black and red details, and it was definitely the closest I

> *"It roared over with a sound like half-a-dozen Harleys. My Dad said, "Don't worry about the noise it makes – it's when the engine stops that you should worry!"'*

had ever been to a flying machine. It blew up on a house on Woodcrest Road, just one street below us, and a few houses to the north. I don't remember seeing the explosion; probably Mother had grabbed me and hugged me to her … We lost our window glass, roof tiles and much else attached to the house.'[4] The V1 which Barry recalled may well have been the one that fell on 17 Woodcrest Road on 3 July 1944. It claimed the lives of the two occupants, 75-year-old William Woodman and his wife, Emma, who was 79.

It was the silence that followed the demise of a V1's engine that people quickly came to dread, as historian Charles Whiting once described: 'All London tensed daily now as they heard that first distant hum, growing to a louder harsh rattle, which either vanished as the "buzz-bomb" flew on or stopped abruptly, followed a few seconds later by the roar of one ton of high explosive detonating. That twelve seconds silence between the engine cutting out and the blast of the explosion seemed to be the hardest part to bear – that tense, electric brooding silence when the same terrifying thought flashed through

everyone's mind: has this one got my number on it?'[5]

The terrifying fear that Whiting referred to very quickly began to take its toll. 'It just seems to be like a colossal and hideous game of spite,' complained Vivienne Hall. 'Just to send these things over haphazardly to make life a chancy unpleasant thing for we long-suffering Londoners … We have had to face up to horrible things for nearly five years, I suppose we shall continue to do so, but, God, how tired we are of it. Just working and living and sleeping though one mad, noisome form of destruction week after week, month after month, without the excitement of battle or the thrill of personal victory, without the knowledge that we count for anything, or that our efforts to keep going are contributing towards the ultimate betterment of conditions in the world.'[6]

Herbert Morrison quickly came to the same conclusions as Hall. 'After five years of war the civilian population were not as capable of standing the strains of air attacks as they had been during the winter of 1940-41. I will do everything to hold up their courage and spirit – but there is a limit ▶

and the limit will come.'

Seemingly, even the Third Reich's Minister of Propaganda, Joseph Goebbels, once summed up the omnipresent nature of the V1: 'The effect of the German bombardment lies in its persistency … I can imagine how, quite apart from the damage it might cause, it would gradually build up on your nerves. It's like toothache. The pain is, of itself, not so bad. But when your tooth aches and throbs all day and all night, then you can't think clearly, in fact all you can do is think about this accursed pain.'[7]

One official account summarized the first few weeks of the flying bomb offensive: 'Half of the two thousand six hundred bombs that had come overland between 13th June and 15th July had fallen in the London area. The physical damage that was caused to essential war factories and vital communications was small; but some fourteen thousand casualties in dead and seriously injured, some thirteen thousand houses irreparably damaged and over half-a-million more or less damaged was no small prize for London and the south-east to pay.

'That the attack was disturbing was natural. There was no certain relief from attack at any hour of the day, in contrast with the almost exclusively night attacks of 1940-41 and the early months of 1944. In addition, the blast effect of the weapon was, seemingly so much more widely spread than in the case of ordinary bombs, and

> *"The alerts increased in frequency to such an extent, notes Juliet Gardiner, that it 'became "like a child pushing a door bell and running away".'*

caused more domestic disturbance. This was one factor which, by increasing the rate of absenteeism, accounted for the definite decline in production in the London area, a decline which, in the case, for example, of the radio industry, amounted to over twenty per cent. The other main factors were loss of time in actual working hours through workers taking shelter, and lowered efficiency through loss of sleep and anxiety …

'So far, no unusual or disturbing effects on morale had become evident; but as the attacks were likely to continue, adding always to the results of the strain under which people were living and working, morale was not likely to improve unless the defences could appreciably reduce the number of bombs that were falling daily upon the capital.'

The alerts increased in frequency to such an extent, notes Juliet Gardiner, that it 'became "like a child pushing

a door bell and running away". An Air Ministry official at work in the Aldwych "counted over 30 alarms in a single day" and often they came so frequently that people found it difficult to remember whether there was an alert on or not.'

Minor incidents often attracted undue attention by nature of the location of the explosion or its unusual circumstances, a fact that the author Philip Ziegler once touched on: 'A V1 which fell in the garden of Buckingham Palace broke a few

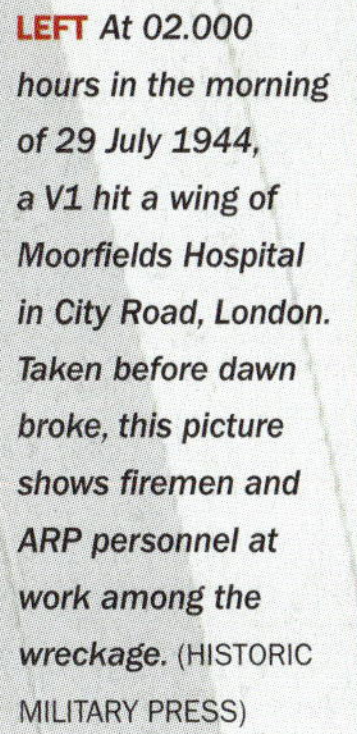

windows, demolished a summerhouse and damaged the tennis court on which George VI had used to play before the war; a bomb on the zoo killed two pheasants and an adder, which died of the cold after the roof of its high-temperature house had been shattered by blast. In Bermondsey, a cereal warehouse was hit and the area around flooded with three feet of grain. A fire started and the firemen's hoses washed the grain into the drains where it swelled and blocked the flow of sewage. An appalling stench and a plague of flies were added to the miseries of those who lived nearby.'[8]

It was the serious flying bomb incidents, however, that would challenge the public's resolve the most. The events which unfolded in the Aldwych on 30 June 1944 provide just one example.

Sweeping in a wide crescent linking the Strand, Fleet Street and Kingsway, the area around the Aldwych was home to a number of important buildings and institutions, including the BBC's Bush House, Adastral House (in which part of the Air Ministry was located), Australia House and the Waldorf Hotel.

The road was busy with office workers out enjoying the summer sunshine, taking their lunch break or even queuing at the local Post Office. At 14.07 hours, a V1, its motor having cut out moments earlier, glided silently in over the Thames, diving down to explode in the road between the Air Ministry and the north-east wing of Bush House. The blast wave scythed down the street, the shock wave ripping through the windows of nearby buildings, shattering the fixtures and fittings within. Many of those out in the open were killed or seriously wounded by a combination of blast or flying glass fragments from the hundreds of shattered windows. Their bodies lay in the street, crumpled up against the walls of buildings where they had been blown by the explosion.

One BBC employee later recalled: 'It was as if a foggy November evening had materialised at the throw of a switch, through the dust and smoke the casement of the bomb lay burning in a corner of Kingsway: three victims lay unmoving at the top of the steps only thirty yards from where we had crouched and huddled figures were ▶

scattered all over the road.'

Derrick Grady was 14½ when he left school in 1944. Having accepted a job as a Post Room boy for the BBC, he was working at Bush House that fateful Friday in June 1944. Like his unidentified colleague previously mentioned, Derrick had luck on his side that day: 'We were returning from our breath of fresh air and as we entered the East court of Bush House we could hear the alarm bells ringing inside the building which meant "enemy action imminent" (The public air raid warning siren had sounded while we were on the Embankment).

'Just as we arrived at the side entrance to the building, we heard the V1 and its engine cut out. One of my friends shouted, "There it is!" and we saw this buzz bomb clearly just above the North East wing of Bush House before it disappeared behind the buildings. We turned and flung ourselves to the ground. I was in mid-air when the blast hit me. I still have no idea why I wasn't hurt.

'When we got to our feet, there were injured people all around us. All my colleagues were unhurt so we started to get people into the building where help was rapidly forthcoming. The Fire Brigade and large numbers of Ambulances seemed to appear in no time. Also, at that time there were other emergency workers who formed Rescue units.

'After some time, I was able to climb the steps which led from the courtyard at Strand level up to Aldwych. This was very near to the point of impact which was just outside the doors leading to a Post Office on the ground floor of the North East wing of Bush

RIGHT *Rescuers at work after a V1 struck a block of flats in Nevern Square, Kensington, at 16.23 hours on Sunday, 23 July 1944. It exploded approximately where the North gate of the square is today, killing two people.* (HISTORIC MILITARY PRESS)

ABOVE *On 15 July 1944, a V1 hit the village of Goodworth Clatford in Hampshire. The explosion destroyed a number of buildings and left six people dead and several more injured. This shelter was built in their memory, whilst a plaque on the inside wall lists the dead.* (COURTESY OF ROBERT MITCHELL)

MIDDLE RIGHT *Londoners take cover from V1s in a deep shelter on 27 July 1944.* (HISTORIC MILITARY PRESS)

ABOVE *The Church of St Mary at Little Chart in Kent was hit by a V1 just after 20.00 hours on the evening of 16 August 1944.* (HISTORIC MILITARY PRESS)

LEFT *The remains of a V1 being removed from the Regent Palace Hotel's Annex, in Brewer Street, London, where it fell at 12.40 hours on 30 June 1944. It struck the north-eastern corner of the Annexe's roof. The single fatality was a chambermaid who was blown out of an upper floor window; 168 were injured.* (HISTORIC MILITARY PRESS)

House. At that time of day, the Post Office was crowded. When I got to the top of the steps the whole area across the junction of Kingsway and Aldwych was covered by occupied stretchers. I asked a Rescue man if he wanted help loading these stretchers on to Ambulances and he said to me, "Not any of these, lad, they won't be going anywhere!" I went and found my jacket which earlier I had put under someone's head. It was covered in blood. I went back to work.'9

A Reuters office boy, running to help, came across a middle-aged woman sitting on the pavement, propped up against a shop front. Her face was deathly white, blood running from lacerations all over her face and neck. One of her shoes was missing and her stockings torn. She had auburn hair and was still clutching her handbag. He bent down to see if he could help her. Then a voice behind him said: 'There's nothing you can do for her, chum. She's gone. Died about two or three minutes ago.'

This, one of the deadliest V1 flying bomb attacks of the war, left forty-six people dead, whilst at least 200 others suffered serious injuries. Included in the casualties were five members of

the Women's Auxiliary Air Force who died on the upper floors of the Air Ministry. The Aldwych incident, though, was just one example of the many such tragedies which played out across the UK between D-Day and the end of the War in Europe, and which, in time, would be worsened by the arrival of another of Hitler's deadly new weapons. ●

NOTES

1 Philip Ziegler, *London at War* (Alfred A. Knopf, New York, 1995), p.289.
2 Quoted on www.levyboy.com/wartime.htm
3 Joan Miller, *One Girl's War* (1970)
4 See Barry Cogswell, *To Have Bourne Witness* (AuthorHouse, Bloomington, 2014).
5 Quoted in Nigel Blundell, 'Terror of the Doodlebugs', *The Daily Express*, 31 May 2014.
6 Juliet Gardiner, *Wartime Britain 1939-1945* (Headline, London, 2004), p.643.
7 Brooks, Geoffrey, *Hitler's Nuclear Weapons*, Leo Cooper, London, 1992.
8 Philip Zieger, ibid.
9 Derrick Grady, 'The Aldwych Buzzbomb', quoted on the WW2 People's War website.

Disaster
at the Guards Chapel

IT WAS ON THE MORNING OF SUNDAY, 18 JUNE 1944, JUST DAYS AFTER THE START OF THE V1 CAMPAIGN, THAT THE UK SUFFERED ITS WORST FLYING BOMB INCIDENT OF THE WAR.

Second Subaltern Elisabeth Sheppard-Jones had good reason to remember the events of Sunday, 18 June 1944, for it was, she later wrote, 'the last day on which I walked'.[1] Serving in the Auxiliary Territorial Service and based in London, that morning Elisabeth had agreed to meet her childhood friend Air Raid Warden Pauline Gye and that the pair should attend the morning service at the Guards' Chapel in Wellington Barracks.

Having made their way across St James's Park, the two of them settled themselves into a pair of seats towards the back of the Chapel. Not long after, with a band of Guardsmen providing the music, the service began.

'We sang the opening hymn,' Elisabeth later recalled in 1958. 'I probably enjoyed that, for my Welsh blood ensures a fondness for hymn singing. My mind must have

ABOVE The ruins of the Guards' Chapel pictured from the area in which Second Subaltern Elisabeth Sheppard-Jones sat for the service. (HISTORIC MILITARY PRESS)

RIGHT The interior of the ruins of the Guards' Chapel looking towards what was the main entrance. (HISTORIC MILITARY PRESS)

wandered during the reading of the first lesson – it usually does. I daresay I was thinking about my forthcoming leave or of what chance I had of getting my third pip. "Here endeth the first lesson," the Guards' Colonel who had been reading it must have said.

'The congregation rose to its feet. I rose to my feet – never to do so again. And this is the clearest part of all. I can see what happened as clearly as I can see the last of the roses outside my window at this moment …

'In the distance hummed faintly the engine of a flying bomb. "We praise thee, O God: we acknowledge Thee to be the Lord," we, the congregation, sang. The dull burr became a roar, through which our voices could now only faintly be heard. "All the earth doth worship Thee: the father everlasting."

'The roar stopped abruptly as the engine cut out. We were none of us then as familiar as later all London and the south was to be become with Hitler's new weapon, to recognise this ominous sign. The *Te Deum* soared again into the silence …

'Then there was a noise so loud it was as if all the waters and the winds in the world had come together in mighty conflict, and the Guards' Chapel collapsed upon us in a bellow of bricks and mortar. There was no time for panic, no time to stretch out a hand to Pauline for comfort. One moment I was singing the *Te Deum*, and the next I lay in dust and blackness, aware of one thing only – that I had to go on breathing.'

Westminster's third V1

That morning the Germans had launched three flying bombs that were soon heading for the heart of London. Until then, with the V1 campaign only a few days old, none of these missiles had landed in the Westminster area. But, on that Sunday, the borough's first bomb landed on Hungerford Bridge in the early hours; the next landed on Carey Mansions in Rutherford Street, demolishing the building. The third bomb to hit the Westminster area was launched just after 11.00 hours. It tipped forward in its terminal dive some twenty minutes later, right above Elisabeth and the rest of the congregation in the Guards' Chapel.

Guardsman Keith Lewis described what happened next: 'It was during the reading of the lesson that it all happened. The Commanding Officer, Lord Edward Hay, was about halfway through the text when we heard the

ABOVE *Looking down on the shell of the devastated Guard's Chapel in Wellington Barracks after most of the rubble from the V1 explosion on Sunday, 18 June 1944 has been cleared away. Nearby blocks of flats, among them Broadway Buildings and Queen Anne's Mansions in Petty France, also suffered blast damage.* (HISTORIC MILITARY PRESS)

by now familiar "motor-cycle-engine" sound of a V1. It became quite loud, but I was sure it would continue on its way to some other unfortunate part of London, as all the others had done so far.

'Suddenly, the engine noise stopped. What happened then was all within a nano of time, although I still see and hear it in sequence thus: a large semi-circular area at the top half of the south wall collapsed; there was an intensive blue flash; I saw the Commanding Officer still standing but backwards at an angle of around 45 degrees. I remember noticing the ash-grey colour of his face (and later, I concluded that he was already dead at this moment); there was a very loud ▶

explosion (again later, I likened it to the loudness of a bang of an AA gun outside in St James' Park); then some giant was hammering me all over my back.'[2] Standing outside, some distance away on the steps of the Officers' Mess, Lieutenant David Gurney watched events unfold: 'At [11.05 hours], the Old Guard …

marched back from Buckingham Palace … and began to dismount on the square. At 11.10 the noise of a buzz bomb was heard approaching and I went on to the front steps to watch. The Captain and Subaltern of the Guard (Robin Barnes-Gorell and Nigel Mitchison) were walking towards the Mess and the Ensign (Peter Daubeny) was dismissing the men. There were about sixty men on the square some 150 yards away from the Chapel.

'At 11.11 the bomb crashed through the roof of the Chapel and exploded inside. I saw the bomb falling and noticed its square cut wings. I threw myself on the ground … A considerable explosion occurred but not one man on the square was touched.'[3]

'Are you alright?'

One witness to the immediate aftermath at the Chapel was none other than Professor R.V. Jones, who had been responsible for much of the analysis of the intelligence on the V1 (and later the V2). This incident was, he later mused, that which 'remains most in my memory'.

'Charles Frank and I were both in the office [at Whitehall],' he

THE BRIGADE OF GUARDS HELD A DRUMHEAD THANKSGIVING SERVICE IN FRONT OF THE GUARDS' CHAPEL, WELLINGTON BARRACKS, WHICH WAS DESTROYED BY A FLYING BOMB IN JUNE LAST YEAR. THE ALTAR WAS ERECTED ON DRUMS.

wrote. 'Shortly after eleven o'clock I was on the telephone to Bimbo Norman at Bletchley when we heard the unforgettable noise of a flying bomb. Norman could hear it over the telephone, too, and then the engine cut out. I remarked to him that this was going to be pretty near, and that we were getting under our desks.

'There was a deafening explosion, and I can remember Norman's voice saying, "Are you alright? Are you alright?", and I assured him that we were. I then went out of the office to see what had happened, and found that the bomb had fallen about 150 yards away on the Guards' Chapel …

'There was nothing for me to do, for the Guards had everything under control, and were already carrying out the dead. But that sight, coupled with the sea of fresh green leaves that had been torn from the plane trees in Birdcage Walk, brought home to me the difference between one ton of explosive in actuality and the one ton that we had predicted in the abstract six months before.'[4]

'Please, please, I'm here'

As Professor Jones had observed, the civil defence services were quickly on the scene – it took, for example, just eight minutes for the first heavy rescue squads to arrive and get to work.

'As the clouds of dust subsided,' notes one account, 'first aid teams and heavy rescue crews arrived to find a scene of utter devastation. An initial City of Westminster ARP assessment put the number of casualties at 400-500. At first, the debris appeared impenetrable; the smashed remains of walls and the collapsed roof had trapped dozens. The doors to the Chapel were blocked; the only access point for the rescue teams lay behind the altar.

Doctors and nurses were obliged to scramble in between the concrete walls to administer morphine and first aid. Several rescuers and survivors later recalled that the silver altar cross had been untouched by the blast and candles continued to burn. The rescue services and Guardsmen from the Barracks immediately began freeing survivors from the wreckage and carrying them out.'[5]

One of those carried out was Second Subaltern Elisabeth Sheppard-Jones: 'I have often been asked since of what I thought during those hours when I lay buried. Did I think I was going to die? And if so, did my past life parade its characters and scenes before me as is said to happen to a drowning person? All I can say is that I didn't think of anything, and yet I know that I was conscious. I felt no pain, I was scarcely aware of the chunks of massed grey concrete that had piled on top of me, nor did I realise that this was why breathing was so difficult. My whole being was concentrated in the one tremendous effort of taking in long struggling breaths and then letting them struggle out again.

'It may have been an hour

later, perhaps two or three or more, that greater consciousness came to me. I was suddenly aware that somewhere far above me, above the black emptiness, there were people, living helpful people whose voices reached me, dim and disembodied as in a dream.

'"Please, please, I'm here," I said, and I went on saying it until my voice was hoarse and my throat ached with the dust that poured down it. To this day I can sometimes smell that acrid dust in my nostrils.'[6] Seriously wounded, Elisabeth was rushed to hospital. Her injuries were so severe that, despite years of treatment and operations, she never walked again. Her friend, Pauline Gye, was killed beside her in the Chapel.

The operation to free everyone from the ruins of the Chapel took forty-eight hours to complete. When the final casualty list was compiled, it was established that 121 soldiers and civilians had been killed, a further 141 were seriously

injured. The death toll included the officiating Chaplain, Revd Ralph Whitrow, several senior British Army officers and a US Army Colonel.

Despite the fact that the days' old V1 campaign had just seen its worst single incident in the UK, the toll of death and destruction would continue for many months. ●

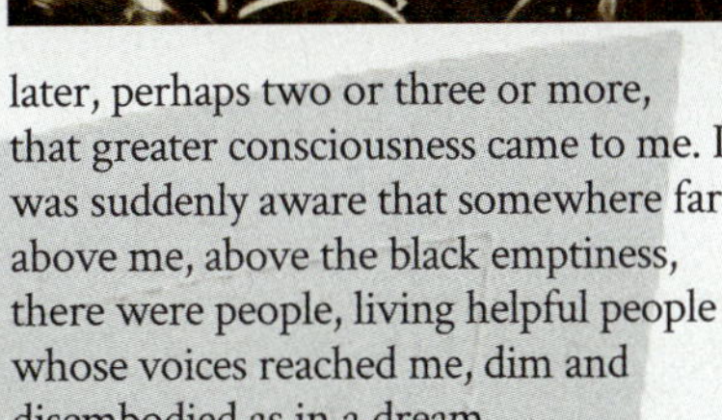

NOTES

1 Elisabeth Sheppard-Jones' graphic account is quoted from her moving autobiography, *I Walk on Wheels* (Geoffrey Bles, London, 1958).

2 Jan Gore, *Send More Shrouds: The V1 Attack on the Guards' Chapel 1944* (Pen & Sword Books, Barnsley, 2017), p. 9.

3 ibid, pp.9-10.

4 R.V. Jones, *Most Secret War* (Hamish Hamilton, London, 1978), p.424.

5 See www.westendatwar.org.uk.

6 Elisabeth Sheppard-Jones, ibid, p.13.

Air-launched Flying Bombs

AS THE ALLIED FORCES OVERRAN THE V1 SKI-SITES THE GERMANS DEVISED A NEW MEANS OF DELIVERING ONE OF HITLER'S VENGEANCE WEAPONS.

By mid-July 1944, most of the V1 ski-sites in northern France had either been destroyed from the air, or overrun by Allied ground forces that had broken out from the Normandy beachhead. The Luftwaffe, though, was not unprepared for this. When the first V1s were tested, they had been launched not from ramps on the ground, but from aircraft in the sky. Already, by the summer of 1944, a Ju 88 unit – II Gruppe/Kampfgeschwader 51 (II./KG 51) – had been withdrawn from the Eastern Front to convert to Heinkel He 111s which could carry V1s.

Redesignated III./KG 3, the unit was equipped with H-16, H-20 and H-22 variants of the He 111, these having the normal bomb stowage removed so that a V1 could be under slung between the fuselage and the engine on the starboard side. In June 1944, the Gruppe moved to a series of bases in northern France, at locations such as Rosières, Amy and Amiens, in preparation for the commencement of its campaign against the UK. However, it is believed that the campaign's start was delayed following a USAAF raid on Beauvais on 16 June 1944, which destroyed and damaged a number of aircraft, and a strafing attack on Plantlünne four days later, which saw at least one He 111 being destroyed and five aircrew and three groundcrew wounded.

BELOW *One of the Heinkel He 111 H-16s of 2./KG 53 that participated in Operation Rumpelkammer. With the Wk Nr 16100, and coded A1+HK, the extent of this aircraft's involvement, and its fate, is not known.* (COURTESY OF CHRIS GOSS)

OPPOSITE PAGE, TOP RIGHT *An air-launched V1 mounted on a Heinkel He 111 H-22.* (HISTORIC MILITARY PRESS)

Operation Rumpelkammer

Under the codename Operation *Rumpelkammer* (Junk Room), the Heinkels finally went into action with their first attack upon London on the night of 3-4 July 1944.[1] This mission was undertaken by a total of fourteen aircraft, all of which returned unscathed. The next attack, also against London, was on the night of 6-7 July. The following night a further mission was flown against the British capital, but on this occasion two He 111s of 9./KG 3, those flown by Unteroffizier Wilhelm Nolte and Unteroffizier Martin Mehnert, collided on the runway at Amy with the total destruction of both aircraft and the death of one crew member. A final attack was delivered from northern France on 9 July, which saw the loss of one aircraft and its five-man crew, before the gruppe moved to Venlo in Holland to escape the continuing advance of the Allied forces.

Moving to The Netherlands had an added advantage in that the Heinkels would be able to avoid the highly effective defences which had been built up around London and the South East. From Venlo, the bombers could fly out over the North Sea to attack from a new direction.

To avoid detection, missions for air-launching the V1 were flown at low-level, as one British report stated: 'A minimum safety height for release is laid down at 500 metres. The aircraft usually flies at a height of 100 metres over the sea and shortly before

BELOW *Crews of III./KG 53 briefing for a V1 sortie. The officer to the right is believed to be Hauptmann Siegfried Jessen, Staffelkapitän of 9./KG 53. Jessen and his crew were shot down on 5 January 1945, having just taken off on a V1 launching mission.* (COURTESY OF CHRIS GOSS)

this was shot down by anti-aircraft fire from a German convoy in the Scheldt Estuary.

Back to Germany

August 1944 would see missions being flown on at least twelve nights involving at least 228 aircraft. This included a raid on 30-31 August, the target that night, unusually, reported as being Gloucester, with twenty V1s being launched in the early morning. Of these, only eight crossed the coast, after which all the flying bombs fell in East Anglia, nowhere near their intended target.

The following month, September, would see similar sporadic operations with a break between 5 and 16 September by which time the gruppe had relocated to Varrelbusch in Germany. Towards dawn on 16 September, however, the attack was resumed. The first flying bomb fell in Essex at 05.49 hours. A few minutes later another came down at Barking. During the next half-hour five more bombs approached England. One of these reached Woolwich whilst

their V1s, and then rapidly descend again to the previous 'wave-top' level for the return flight. This low altitude flying accounted for Unteroffizier Günter Rohne and his crew from 9./KG 3 when they hit an aerial mast near Eindhoven on a mission to London on 27 July.

By the end of July 1944, it is believed that III./KG 3 had flown over 360 V1 sorties on at least eighteen different nights, between them launching at least 280 V1s. The effectiveness of these attacks is, however, hard to assess due to a lack of documentary evidence and the fact that these early air-launching sorties were mixed in with conventional V1 launches. Losses among the Heinkels were also mounting, with four aircraft being lost during a single mission against London on 29 July. The next night saw the loss of another Heinkel, but

> *"Under the codename Operation Rumpelkammer (Junk Room), the Heinkels finally went into action with their first attack upon London on the night of 3-4 July 1944."*

another fell at Felsted; the remaining three were brought down by fighters, one of them into the sea. Two flying bombs not included in these figures were destroyed at sea by the Royal Navy.

In the region of thirteen nights of attacks took place in September with a total of 177 missiles being despatched, predominantly against London. Until this date, losses among the bombers had been primarily due to accidents or anti-aircraft fire but in September RAF night fighters started to make an impression. First blood was a He 111 probably destroyed over the North Sea by Flying Officer Ray Henley of ▶

release the pilot makes height to 500 metres or 100 metres higher than the minimum laid down.' This, in fact, over simplifies the method used by the German pilots.

The aircrews developed a tactic called 'lo-hi-lo' in which the Heinkels would, upon leaving their airbases and crossing the coast, descend to an exceptionally low altitude. When the launch point was neared, the bombers would swiftly ascend, fire

ABOVE *Hauptmann Jessen's He 111 was shot down by a 406 Squadron Mosquito. The pilot of the Mosquito, Squadron Leader (later Wing Commander) Russ Bannock, is seen here on the left.* (COURTESY OF CHRIS GOSS)

Groet killing all the crew. Another aircraft was lost on 8 October, though surprisingly no losses were recorded during a large raid of twenty Heinkels in two waves on the night of 8-9 October.

Missions against London continued for another ten nights until 19 October, with the RAF making no claims for He 111s. However, two aircraft from 7 and 8 Staffel collided on 9 October and crashed near Leeuwarden with the deaths of all ten aircrew, whilst on 14 October another Heinkel crashed on landing at Münster-Handorf returning from an attack against London. The final loss

25 Squadron at 21.50 hours on the 24th of the month, which was followed nearly seven hours later with a similar claim by Wing Commander Leicester Mitchell also of 25 Squadron.

To meet the threat from this new direction, Pile and Hill decided to extend the existing anti-aircraft defences northwards from the London area by adding a 'Diver Strip' extending from the left flank of the defences at Clacton up to Great Yarmouth. A few guns had already been moved northwards from the belt near the South Coast and it was decided to carry this process a stage further. Between 16 and 19 September orders were issued to sixteen heavy and nine light anti-aircraft batteries to move from the belt to the coast between Clacton and Harwich. As the month went on further moves were introduced, so much so that by the middle of October no less than 498 heavy and 609 light anti-aircraft guns were deployed to counter the air-launched V1s.

As well as more V1s being destroyed as they crossed the coast, German

> *"The aircraft usually flies at a height of 100 metres over the sea and shortly before release the pilot makes height to 500 metres or 100 metres higher than the minimum laid down."*

aircraft losses continued to creep up, with Wing Commander Mitchell, for example, claiming two more He 111s early in the morning of 29 September. One of these was that flown by Oberleutnant Erhard Banneick, who was the Staffelkapitän of 9./KG 3. The following night, the Staffelkapitän of 7./KG 3 was killed in an air raid on Münster-Handorf airfield, which meant that all three Staffelkapitän of III./KG 3 had now been killed in action in the space of six days. The value of these V1 attacks, the results of which were uncertain, compared with the losses of highly experienced air crew was certainly questionable at best. Nevertheless, the operations continued.

The attacks recommenced from Varrelbusch and Ahlhorn on 5 October, with London yet again marked out as the target for eleven aircraft, all of which returned safely bar one.

Eleven aircraft also struck at London on the evening of 7 October. During this *Rumpelkammer* attack, the Heinkel flown by Feldwebel Lothar Gall of 8./KG 3 collided with a radio mast at Petten and crashed into a house at

for III./KG 3 was the He 111 flown by Oberfeldwebel Werner Schmidt-Reich of 8 Staffel who failed to return.

Increased effort

Though the V1 attacks upon the UK were quite clearly having no impact upon Allied strategy, as evidenced by the consolidation of the Allied forces on the borders of the Reich, rather than draw back every resource to defend Germany, on 20 October

Rumpelkammer was expanded when III./KG 3 was joined by Major Herbert Wittmann's II./KG 53, with III./KG 3 being redesignated I./KG 53.

This increased force raised concerns in London, and an immediate reponse was called for, with new methods for the early detection of the V1s being tried. One such effort was that recalled by Spitfire pilot Flight Lieutenant Geoff Richards: 'In November 1944 Fighter Command rang me and asked if I would volunteer for a special mission. I was to operate a small radar set in the back of a Wellington. Three Mosquitoes were to follow me in line astern at 200 feet off the Dutch coast as at that time the Germans were launching V1s from He 111s halfway across the North Sea. We were to intercept and destroy. It didn't work!'

It is likely that Richards was involved in the system described in the following account: 'To assist in detecting the Heinkels the Fighter Interception Development Squadron borrowed a Coastal Command Wellington equipped with a modified ASV Mk VI radar set and PPI [Plan Position Indicator – a type of radar] to act as Airborne Early Warning and Control. After trials, low level night patrols off the north of the Netherlands were carried out by the Wellington with several Mosquito night fighters. For the night fighters to locate and keep station with the

Wellington, the aircraft was fitted with a special homing beacon.'

Other schemes were tried, but all had only limited success. The only certain way that the Heinkels could be stopped was by using more fighters to intercept them. This took the form of 68 Squadron, the newly-created Fighter Interception Development Squadron (FIDS) equipped with Beaufighters, and Nos. 125, 307 and 456 squadrons which were operating Mosquitoes.

Apart from two accidents on 21 and 23 October, the first German losses for FIDS (which was operating under the codename *Vapour*) occurred on 25-26 October 1944, when one of its pilots, Flying Officer Desmond Tull, and Flying Officer Bill Beadle of 125 Squadron each claimed a He 111 off Lowestoft and Yarmouth respectively.

Another Heinkel was lost on 31 October, being brought down over the North Sea by Squadron Leader Bill Gill of 125 Squadron: 'Gave the He 111 another long burst from 1,000 feet range and obtained many strikes all on the starboard side of the fuselage. This set aircraft alight and it went straight down into the sea. From a quick glance there appeared to be no survivors.'

Though November 1944 started quietly, by the 6th of the month II./KG 53 had lost nine aircraft on operations, with two more crashing in Holland on their return. To further add to the Germans' problems, their bases were subjected to raids by Bomber Command and the USAAF's Eighth Air Force.

In a bid to counter the increasingly effective anti-aircraft and RAF defences on Christmas Eve 1944, about fifty Heinkels – almost the entire operational strength of the air-launching unit – were despatched on Operation *Martha*. Having headed out over the North Sea, the bomber crews launched bombs in the direction of Manchester from positions off the coast between Skegness and Bridlington.

The first people to directly witness the launchings, aside from a ▶

RIGHT *Heinkel killers of 125 Squadron. Squadron Leader Bill Gill is seated far left, whilst Flying Officer Bill Beadle is in the first row of standing men, seventh from the right.* (COURTESY OF CHRIS GOSS)

MIDDLE RIGHT *This crater was caused by the air-launched V1 that fell at Clough House Farm, near Five Ashes, three miles east of Macclesfield, on Christmas Eve 1944.* (COURTESY OF COLIN PARK; WWW. GEOGRAPH.ORG.UK)

BELOW *The Beaufighter VIF, V8565 coded ZQ-F, which was flown by Squadron Leader Jeremy Howard-Williams, of the Fighter Interception Development Squadron, when he claimed a He 111 on 4 November 1944.* (MRS J. HOWARD-WILLIAMS, VIA ANDREW THOMAS)

number of radar operators, were the crews of several trawlers out at sea. 'Skipper Gorringe of the trawler *Gurth*, fishing several miles south-east of the Dowsing Spar buoy,' notes one author, 'saw one successful and four or five failed launchings. Skipper Miller of the *Scout*, fishing fourteen miles north-east of 62B buoy, saw up to eighteen, mainly to the north-west of his position. He saw at least one bomb go into the sea.'[2]

The launches took place over a period of about an hour between 05.00 hours and 06.00 hours. Pile, though, had prepared for just such an eventuality. Just in case the Lufwaffe tried to fly their V1s further north, he had devised a scheme where fifty-nine batteries of guns could be rapidly deployed between Skegness and Whitby if an attack should develop in that area.

The RAF also played its usual vigilent part. Flight Sergeant A. Bullus

and his observer, Flying Officer T.W. Edwards, were at the controls of their 68 Squadron Mosquito XVII TA389 – just one of the many patrols airborne that night. Once the bombers were picked up by radar, Bullus and Edwards were vectored onto one target by Orby radar control. A visual sighting was soon made, and Bullus fired three two-second bursts: 'The first at 200ft struck the starboard wing root, the second at 100ft the fuselage and the third at 50ft the port engine and wing root. The target burst into flames, did an uncontrolled climbing turn to port and peeled into the sea, where it was observed to be on fire for at least five minutes.'[3]

Depsite the defenders' best efforts, thirty V1s came within range of the reporting system during Operation *Martha*, and all thirty crossed the coast. One of these missles that had flown on inland reached as far as

Tottington, a small town between Bury and Ramsbottom on the edge of the West Pennine Moors. There its engine fell silent, tipping the flying bomb down towards the ground. At

05.50 hours it hit a row of terraced houses in Chapel Street, killing seven people and injuring fourteen others – the second worst incident of the operation. Rescue workers toiled for over ten hours in an effort to bring out the survivors and the dead.

One resident of Tottington who later recalled the events that night was Colin MacDonald, who was aged 14 at the time: 'I just woke up with a tremendous bang and the ceiling coming in on top of the bed. There was a mad scramble to get out. We didn't know what happened. We thought it might be a gas explosion. None of us thought it would be a bomb or a flying bomb. We got out and all the backs of the houses were down and there was a crater, 30ft deep, and all the windows were out. There was glass from kerb to kerb.'[4]

Only one of the V1s launched that night actually reached Manchester itself, but six came down within ten miles of the centre of the city and eleven within fifteen miles.

There was a spread of 170 miles from the northernmost bomb at Spennymoor in County Durham, and the southernmost at Woodford in Northamptonshire. Thirty-seven people were killed and sixty-seven seriously injured.

WASTED RESOURCES

The Christmas Eve attack was the last hurrah for II./KG 53. The final air-launched flying-bomb to reach the UK came down at Hornsey at 02.13 hours on 14 January 1945.

While each V1 that struck a house or killed an innocent civilian was in itself a tragedy, the air-launched flying bombs had no material effect upon the outcome of the war. Following the resumption of the Heinkel operations on 16 September 1944 until 14 January 1945 only 576 V1s reached the coast without being shot down into the sea by fighters or the Royal Navy. Of these, 321 were brought down by anti-aircraft fire. One hundred and ninety-seven of these fell into the sea and the remaining 124 on land.

The men of Kampfgeschwader 3 had paid a heavy price for little return. Somewhat puzzled by the persistence of the Luftwaffe in continuing with these unprofitable attacks, which were causing the Germans such high casualty rates, Frederick Pike suggested that 'the Germans seem to have remained unaware how small a proportion of the bombs launched were reaching London, or else to have resigned themselves to receiving a poor return for their efforts so long as some sort of offensive could be continued against this country'. ●

NOTES

1 Some sources state the attack took place the previous night.
2 Peter J.C. Smith, *Air-launched Doodlebugs: The Forgotten Campaign* (Pen & Sword Books, Barnsley, 2006), pp. 153-4.
3 ibid, p.155.
4 Quoted in the *Bury Times*, 31 December 2013.

TODAY

Aeroplane is still providing the best aviation coverage around. With focus on iconic military aircraft from the 1930s to the 1960s.

shop.keypublishing.com/amsubs

Classic Military Vehicle is the best-selling publication in the UK dedicated to the coverage of all historic military vehicles.

shop.keypublishing.com/cmvsubs

ng.com

Britain's V1 Site

DOWN A LEAFY LANE IN THE HEART OF THE PLEASANT LITTLE CHANNEL ISLAND OF ALDERNEY, REVEALS JOHN GREHAN, LIES A NETWORK OF TUNNELS THAT COULD WELL HIDE A DARK SECRET.

ABOVE *The southern junction of the eastern tunnel complex.* (COURTESY OF TONY MARGIOCCHI)

Set deep in the heart of Alderney, not far from St Anne's, the island's only town, is to be found a network of tunnels dug into the hillside along a valley called Le Val Reuters. Long assumed to be nothing more than ammunition storage shelters or possibly electricity generating stations, the true purpose of the complex was unknown. That was until two military men, John Weigold and Colonel Richard Kemp, decided to explore the tunnels and see if, with their knowledge and experience, they could work out why such a large and unusual construction project had been undertaken by the Germans on so small an island.

When the Germans invaded the Channel Islands in June 1940, only a proportion of the islanders evacuated to mainland Britain. Most had to stay and endure enemy occupation for the rest of the war. The island of Alderney, however, was almost completely abandoned with virtually every family being moved to the mainland. As a result, very little is known about what really took place on what has been called the 'silent island'.

In an effort to understand what the intended purpose was for the tunnels at Le Val Reuters, the two former soldiers set about systematically measuring and recording the main tunnels which are still accessible, though admittedly with some difficulty. The complex itself is split into two parts, a similar pattern being repeated on each side of the valley, with the east tunnel system being the one examined in greatest details. Weigold and Kemp found that there is a downhill gradient from the south entrance to the north, so they assumed that three of the four tunnels in each half were used for storage, and that the fourth was kept clear to allow movement along its length. It is obvious that the tunnels were built for a particular purpose, so the nature of their construction would be the greatest indicator of their intended use.

The tunnels were excavated in a square shape which was, on average, 2.7 metres high and just over 3 metres wide, with only very slight variations throughout. The tunnels were elaborately lined, with a bitumen sheet covering up the walls and across the roof being held in place with thin wooden battens. Over this was laid wooden planks that were 20cm wide and 5cm thick. These were supported in place by trunks of approximately 15cm diameter pinned together at the corners by 35cm iron staples. The tunnels were completely lined, including the flat ends. Electric lights were installed along the entire lengths. All the bends are gradual, and the junctions angled to allow the passage of an 8m long object – a fact that was tested.

Railway tracks are present from the entrance right to the end of each tunnel, the gauge of which is 67cm, with sleepers 57cm apart. There is a drainage channel below each railway. Two of the storage bays are perfectly rendered in thick concrete, rather than the standard cement, to a fine smooth finish unseen anywhere else and which remains in virtually perfect condition. The large east chamber is 23m long, 4.6m wide and 5m high.

The west chamber is 24.5m long, 3m wide and 3m high. Rail lines extend right to the end walls.

Having established the dimensions and nature of the tunnels, the two men began to consider what military objects would require such a structure. They could not be the oft suggested ammunition stores. The junctions, unexpected curves and gentle bends do not correspond to the simple, straight lines and efficient use of space that would normally be expected in a conventional military storage tunnel. Nor could this be a fuel dump or, as has been proposed, an electricity generating station as there are no large spaces for the machinery and there was no adequate ventilation. After considering all other options, and after investigating sites in northern France, the most likely outcome was that this was to be a V1 launch site.

There was, though, one drawback, which was that the completed V1s were too wide. However, examination of technical drawings of the ▶

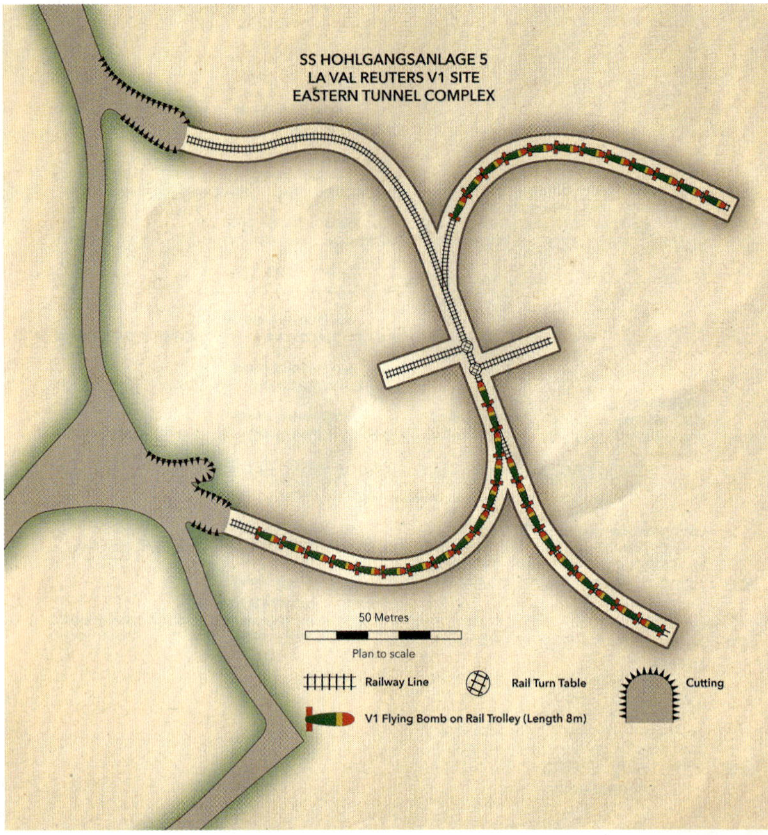

RIGHT *An illustration of how the eastern complex at Le Val Reuters may have appeared.* (COURTESY OF JOHN WEIGOLD)

BOTTOM LEFT
Looking south along the main tunnel of the eastern complex between the storage tunnel entrances. Richard Kemp can be seen in the middle distance. (COURTESY OF TONY MARGIOCCHI)

BOTTOM CENTRE
A flooded rail track in the north-east storage tunnel of the eastern complex. (COURTESY OF TONY MARGIOCCHI)

V1 showed that the wings were detachable, made of plywood and added to the steel fuselage only just before launch. The V1s would have fitted perfectly into the tunnels.

Adolf Island

Let us then look deeper into the possibility that Alderney was the location of a flying bomb launch site. In 1941, Hitler ordered the Channel Islands to be fortified and a massive construction programme was put in hand. On Alderney, four large camps were erected (as well as a number of smaller ones). One of the four, Lager Borkum, housed volunteer workers from Germany, the Netherlands, France and Belgium, who were employed by Organisation Todt. The other three – Lager Helgoland, Lager Norderney and Lager Sylt – were forced or slave labour camps, where prisoners mostly from Russia, Poland and the Ukraine were held. With these bodies of workers, at least 10,000 in total, Alderney, which Hitler gave the codename *Adolf*, was turned into not just the most powerfully defended of all the Channel Islands but one of the most fortified places in the world, and for good reason, as this little island,

just three miles long by one and a half wide, was to serve a very special purpose.

As already mentioned, details of what happened on Alderney are sketchy at best, with only a handful of islanders to observe and report and few of the slave labourers having survived to tell their stories. There is, though, ample evidence, of a very solid form. The fortifications of Alderney were far more extensive than necessary for purely defensive purposes. Had that been the case, Alderney would have been fortified to the same extent as the rest of the archipelago, but the island was six times more densely fortified than either Jersey or Guernsey.

A report by MI.19, which was responsible for obtaining information from enemy prisoners of war, provides a little information about these tunnels: 'These are 14 feet high and wide enough for lorries … The tunnels are always guarded, although well hidden by trees, their entrances are camouflaged by netting.'

A concrete road was built, wide enough for two lines of traffic which led to the tunnels from the harbour and was defended along its length by gun installations. The interrogations by MI.19 revealed that there were some thirty to thirty-five telephone lines which disappeared underground. The interrogations also revealed the high degree of security enforced by the SS – even to the extent that Himmler, the head of the SS – ordered that in the event of an attempt by the Allies to liberate Alderney, all the prisoners were to be executed. The truth about the Alderney site was never to be disclosed.[1]

> *"Alderney, which Hitler gave the codename* Adolf, *was turned into not just the most powerfully defended of all the Channel Islands but one of the most fortified places in the world."*

In February 1943, operational command of Alderney was switched from St Malo on the French coast — from where the Channel Islands as a whole were run — to a different headquarters in Cherbourg. Alderney was, in effect, being isolated from the rest of the islands. Then, in March 1943, Lager Norderney and Lager Sylt were taken over by the SS under the control of Hauptsturmführer Maximilian List. Sylt was turned into a concentration camp – the only one ever created on British soil. This date is significant, as it was also in the spring of 1943 that work began on the V weapons sites in France.

The raid upon Peenemünde and those upon the numerous V weapons sites indicated to the German leaders that either through aerial observation or the activities of the various Resistance movements, the Allied air forces were informed about the locations of the V1 and V2 establishments. Ideally, the Germans needed a place that was within striking distance of London and the English south coast which could be completely sealed from the outside world and one which the RAF and USAAF would refrain from bombing. Finding such a place sounds impossible; Bomber Command and the Eight Air Force had demonstrated that they were prepared to strike anywhere in Western Europe and did not hesitate to attack civilian as well as military targets. Yet there were places where the Allied bombers were reluctant to bomb, for they were part of the British Isles – the Channel Islands.

The RAF conducted a few bombing attacks upon targets across the Channel Islands, but these were mostly against workers of Organisation Todt and harbours being used by the Germans. The risk of hitting civilians or damaging their property was too great for any heavy bombing to be undertaken.

The need to have a site which could be completely sealed was easily found in the island of Alderney, which, as we have seen, had been almost totally abandoned in 1940.

The third requirement, for a location which was within striking distance of the south of England was, of course, easily met, as Alderney is the most northerly of the Channel Islands and only sixty-four miles from Weymouth and around ninety from Southampton. Alderney was therefore the most perfect site that could be found for the deployment of V1s.

The dimensions of the tunnels also proved to be compatible with those being used to house V1s. With an allowance for the wooden lining, the tunnels were almost identical in height and width to the inside of a standard ski site shelter which is 2.73 metres high and 2.8 metres wide. This, in turn, would give the exact lengths needed for three lines of twelve V1s, making a total of thirty-six of the flying bombs. ▶

ABOVE *Surviving gate posts at what was the main entrance to Lager Sylt on Alderney.* (HISTORIC MILITARY PRESS)

ABOVE RIGHT
Located on the wall of the long concrete storage bay, this inscription by a Russian prisoner of war from SS Bauer Brigade 1 confirms that the tunnels were built and completed by this unit by June 1943. (COURTESY OF JOHN WEIGOLD)

RIGHT *A photograph showing the tunnel lining construction, waterproof sheet, thin wood battens and thick wooden planks.* (COURTESY OF TONY MARGIOCCHI)

Other bits of evidence also began to fall into place the more Weigold and Kemp looked. Outside the tunnel, at one side of the valley, was a vast embankment of earth and rock that, at first glance, seemed to be no more than the haphazard dumping of spoil from the original excavation. Except that we could see there was nothing haphazard about this at all.

The landscape had been deliberately altered to create a slope leading up from the tunnel's exit to a specially flattened area with clearance over the surrounding high ground – a perfect site for the 50-metre metal ramps from which V1s were launched. From an old map, they discovered that there had once been a large water tank there, also built by the Germans but for no apparent reason. From their visits to V1 sites in northern France the two men knew this was a vital feature of every V1 launch site, where copious amounts of water were needed close by so the ramps could be washed down between firings to cleanse them of the chemicals used in the launch process.

Sarin gas

Aerial photography taken by a Spitfire of 541 Squadron on 12 June 1944 shows just how extensive the building site at Le Val Reuters was - far greater than anything else on the island. That it was a V weapon facility is certain, but the remarkably fine finish of two of the tunnels seems far too good for simple V1s. There would be no need for such perfection. What reason could there be for so much care to be taken deep underground? The answer to this question might be revealed by the testimony of one of the very few eyewitnesses to events on Alderney – a fisherman from Guernsey – who told British intelligence, most likely in 1943, that a batch of 300 or 400 large, yellow-painted containers had been seen being unloaded from a supply ship in the harbour at Alderney. Yellow was (and still is) a colour coding for chemical weapons.

The same witness also reported that the German garrison on Alderney had frequent gas drills, often remaining in their masks for a whole day at a time. Even the heads of their horses, but not those of the prisoners, were covered on these occasions.

It seems highly likely that these two tunnels contained a workroom and storage for chemical warheads, possibly containing the deadly nerve agents Tabun or Sarin, for the V1s. Fortunately, the Normandy invasion came before the Alderney site could be brought into use, being abandoned in June 1944. Had Hauptsturmführer List and those working for him been able to despatch V1s with chemical warheads to the invasion ports where thousands of Allied troops were assembled, Operation *Overlord* might have been in serious jeopardy.

We have seen earlier that the possible use of gas had been mentioned by Churchill. Little could he have realised just how close to the truth he might have been. ●

NOTE

1 TNA, WO 106 5248B SHAEF intelligence directives.

'Like a Clap of Thunder'

AFTER THE HORRORS OF THE FLYING BOMBS CAME THE MOST TERRIFYING MISSILE
OF THEM ALL – THE V2 ROCKET.

At a Press conference regarding the German V1 campaign held on 7 September 1944, Duncan Sandys gave an account of the defeat of Hitler's terror weapon. 'Except possibly for a few last shots,' the Member of Parliament for Norwood declared triumphantly, 'the Battle of London is over'.[1] This was primarily because the ski sites in northern France had been overrun by Allied ground forces which had broken out from the Normandy beaches after D-Day and had captured the V1 launch sites.

ABOVE The aftermath of the first V2 rocket to explode on British soil. This Big Ben incident, No.1, occurred at Staveley Road in Chiswick on 8 September 1944. (HISTORIC MILITARY PRESS)

It was at 18.43 hours the very next day, at which point Sandys' speech had barely been reported, that Londoners, so familiar with the sound of detonating bombs and mines, heard an explosion unlike any they had experienced previously. It was a sound described as 'like a clap of thunder'.

Professor R.V. Jones, who had done so much important work on Hitler's new weapons, later recalled the

been about to cross the road … Eight houses on either side were completely wrecked and many more were severely damaged.'

Following the blast at Staveley Road the government, anxious to prevent alarm and panic among Londoners, immediately implemented its plans for a news blackout concerning the new German weapon. As the author Ian

very moment he realised that the enemy campaign had taken a new turn: 'The papers for Friday 8th September therefore came out with headlines and pictures showing Mr Sandys proclaiming the end of the battle. At twenty minutes to seven that evening Charles Frank and I were in our office when there was a double bang; he and I looked at one another and said almost simultaneously, "That's the first one!" To mock the day's headlines, the V-2 had arrived.'[2]

This, the first V2 rocket to fall on British soil, had exploded in Staveley Road, Chiswick. It was marked up as Big Ben incident No.1 – 'Big Ben' being the codename then applied to long-range rocket attacks. It was followed just sixteen seconds later by Big Ben No.2, which exploded at Parn Wood, Epping. Three people were killed and twenty injured, ten seriously, at Chiswick; but there were no casualties at Epping.

Unaware of what had happened, people were puzzled. There had been no air raid siren and no enemy aircraft seen in the sky. Neither had there been heard the instantly recognisable spluttering of a doodlebug, and, anyway, Duncan Sandys had said that the danger to London had passed.

The *Daily Express* echoed the bewilderment of its readers. 'What happened on 8 September?' The paper asked. 'It was early evening when the whole of London was startled by two terrific explosions. In Staveley Road, Chiswick, the men were taking an evening stroll to the local. Someone was practising scales on the piano in the front room. The women were gossiping at the garden gates. Some others were listening to the radio

RIGHT *Rescue personnel at the scene of Big Ben incident No.162 at the north end of Tottenham Lane in Hornsey, London. The rocket exploded at 08.15 hours on 10 November 1944. The bomb site is today the site of a YMCA fitness centre.* (HISTORIC MILITARY PRESS)

RIGHT *Another view of the aftermath of Big Ben incident No.162 in Hornsey. The building in the background on the right still stands in Tottenham Lane, whilst Hornsey railway station is just out of view around the bend to its left.* (HISTORIC MILITARY PRESS)

… "We heard no sound before the explosion rocked the ground", said the bewildered people in the district. "There was absolutely no warning like the whistle of a bomb or the chug of a flying bomb engine. We did not see anything either." …

'A yawning crater 15 feet deep and 30 feet wide opened where a man had

Jones MBE wrote, at 'Staveley Road onlookers and reporters had gathered at the edge of the cordons. Some seem to have been told that a gas main had exploded, although a few, particularly the reporters, were not convinced and soon stories were being filed with the editors of their newspapers about a new missile. They immediately

submitted them to the censor, most of them knowing what the outcome would be before the stories reached the government offices. Nothing was to be reported, but everyone knew this news blackout could not be sustained for long.

'Over the next few days a succession of missiles with their familiar trademark double bang hit the capital. There then followed a slightly ridiculous period when rumours spread like wildfire by word of mouth and almost everyone knew or guessed that some new rocket weapon had arrived, but nobody admitted it publicly. There was much gossip about the mysterious explosions that were echoing across the capital. Loyal citizens, not wishing to adopt a defeatist attitude, talked of ammunition dumps, delayed-action bombs, long-range shelling by German ships, gasometers and even large boilers exploding. Of all the explanations, the exploding gasometer was the one that was tacitly encouraged by the authorities.'[3]

There were soon so many 'flying gas-mains' that it became a joke among Londoners whenever they heard a bang. As the V2s continued to fall, albeit at a much lower rate than the V1s, it became increasingly obvious that the secrecy surrounding the rockets was beginning to be counterproductive and making people cynical about the reasons for the total news blackout. In one case, at an explosion in Walthamstow, when the Regional Commissioner enquired about the time of the incident, he was contemptuously told by a Civil Defence worker, 'The delayed action bomb fell at 04.45 hours sir'.[4]

The popular British novelist and author A.P. Herbert, then serving as a Royal Navy Petty Officer, would also recall the secrecy at this stage of the V2 campaign: 'The first "bangs", it was whispered officially, were caused by exploding gas-mains or delayed-action bombs. Presently, so many gas-mains

RIGHT *This is the general area in which a V2 exploded at 18.54 hours on 17 December 1944. It shows the junction of Albany Road (the turning on the left) and Bagshot Street in Camberwell, South London. This was Big Ben incident No.363. The rocket fell on open ground on the west side of Bagshot Street, demolishing a factory and twenty-five terraced houses. The blast damaged buildings within a radius of 400 yards. The initial death toll was twelve, though some of the wounded died later in hospital. The area of the explosion is totally transformed today as it forms part of Burgess Park, on the right; rebuilt houses can be seen on the left. Some of the original houses that survived the blast can be seen in the distance.* (COURTESY OF ROBERT MITCHELL)

MIDDLE RIGHT

Looking down on the damage that resulted from a V2 which exploded in Mackenzie Road, Islington, London N7, on the evening of 26 December 1944. Sixty-eight people were killed, eighty-six severely injured and 182 slightly injured. (VIA HISTORIC MILITARY PRESS)

LEFT *A Policeman inspects the remains of a V2 rocket, probably an airburst, during 1944/45.* (VIA HISTORIC MILITARY PRESS)

were exploding that it became a Metropolitan joke: but it was not till 2 January 1945 that the brutal word "rocket" crept even into our confidential "log". Always, before that, it was "bang" or "big bang".

'The V-2, no doubt, was intended to be still more terrifying than the V-1, because there was no warning: but, for that very reason, I think, it was not. No warning is better than continual menace. You did not have to watch one across the sky and wonder where it would fall. There was a sudden bang, a slow column of smoke, and ruin in some small street: but, unless you were near that street, you forgot about it.'[5]

George Orwell, already bombed out of one home by a V1, penned the

> *"The V-2, no doubt, was intended to be still more terrifying than the V-1, because there was no warning: but, for that very reason, I think, it was not. No warning is better than continual menace."*

following thoughts on the V2 for the edition of *Tribune* published on 1 December 1944: 'People are complaining of the sudden unexpected wallop with which these things go off. "It wouldn't be so bad if you got a bit of warning" is the usual formula. There is even a tendency to talk nostalgically of the days of the V1. The good old doodlebug did at least give you time to get under the table, etc. etc. Whereas, in fact, when the doodlebugs were actually dropping, the usual subject of complaint was the uncomfortable waiting period before they went off. Some people are never satisfied.'"

The Fleet Street journalist C. Jory also once considered the lack of warning surrounding the V2: 'It is a strange way of living, when quite ▶

BELOW *On 9 February 1945, a V2 rocket hit Church House in Tavistock Place, London, killing ten people. From the official list of Big Ben occurrences, this was incident No.709, the explosion happening at 16.08 hours. The total casualties, including those at the church, were thirty-four dead and 121 injured. This is a view of the church that was rebuilt in 1955 and 1956.* (COURTESY OF ROBERT MITCHELL)

TOP RIGHT *This plaque that commemorates the dead at Church House during Big Ben incident No.709.* (COURTESY OF ROBERT MITCHELL)

feasibly one may be dead next minute, next hour, or to-morrow with no warning and no escape … a slaying that is purely a matter of luck.'[6]

Working at a factory making woollen garments for the armed forces, the following account by an unidentified V2 victim illustrates just how the rockets could arrive anywhere, at any time – in this case in Leyton:

'I remember saying to a girl on the next machine, "I hope my date turns up tonight. He's a GI and I could do with a pair of nylons or a bar of candy." All of a sudden there was an almighty explosion and I felt a terrible pain in my back. There was silence for a time, then I could hear girls screaming. The next thing I remember was one of the men picking me up and carrying me through the glass and debris.

'We had caught the full blast. It had fallen on a row of houses opposite. I remember a lorry taking us injured girls to the Connaught Hospital, where it was full of injured people, mostly women and children, from the houses. When I came out of my daze, I realized I had a big hole in my left calf which was pouring with blood and a nurse put a bowl under my foot to catch the blood. I heard someone say, "She's got glass in her back", and the next thing I knew I was lying on a table.

'There was a doctor there and nurses and other injured people and then to my horror someone was just ripping all my clothes off, which were soaked with blood. To me, at nineteen years of age, that seemed almost as bad as the injury. I had to lie down on my front while the doctor stitched me up. My back was gashed by glass … I have never felt so much pain in my life.

'They had to do it without freezing it or anything. A nurse gave me her hand to grip, but the tears just rolled out of my eyes. I said to the doctor, "I'm sorry, I don't mean to cry, but I can't help it." He said, "Don't worry … You're being a brave girl. Now we'll do your leg, but that won't hurt quite so much because that's not quite as bad as your back." … I was off work for about a month, and although I still have my scars to remind me, I consider myself very lucky to be alive.'[7]

The Crooked Billet

Every V2 that reached and exploded over the UK, whether an air-burst or on the ground, resulted in varying outcomes in terms of both the scale of death and injury through to the damage to property. For the residents of Bickley in the London Borough of Bromley, Sunday, 19 November 1944, was a cold, dark night with very low cloud and drizzle. There was no street lighting, for this was wartime, and the houses were blacked out. Many residents of this pleasant community were enjoying a dance night in the Crooked Billet public house when disaster struck at 21.18 hours. It was then that Big Ben incident No.219 unleashed its destructive effects on this part of South-East London.

Young Raymond Wattenbach was standing in the dormitory of Bickley Hall School with his back to the window. He saw a light reflected in a wardrobe mirror, descending quite slowly until it disappeared from view. He may have been the only person to see the missile before it crashed into the ground, the whole school

being shaken to its foundations.

At 9 Sunray Avenue, 17-year-old Bernard Pepper was in the living room, where he and his father were reading whilst his mother knitted. 'We experienced a tremendously loud "whooshing" noise and within half a second Mum and I were under the table, closely followed by Dad. After a second or two, the whole house seemed to lift up and drop down again, as if on a giant wave. We didn't hear an explosion and we were left puzzled by the cause.'

When the V2 impacted at Bickley, 11-year-old Sheila Mitchell was

dance hall, which was at the back of our house. Suddenly, there was a very big explosion, followed by complete silence, followed by the noise of the rocket engine (sounding like a modern jet engine) … We could hear the screams of people and heavy debris, including large pieces of concrete from the pub car park, thrown over the pub roof to land on our houses.'

Next door, at 4 Parkfield Way, Stanley Pilcher was walking downstairs when the rocket hit. 'I remember the sudden blast, and all the windows

injured. I was later told that friends of ours, named Les and Ada Draper, pulled me out of the rubble and by so doing probably saved my life, as there was a subsequent further collapse of the structure around us.'[8]

In total twenty-six people were killed at the time of the explosion. A further victim, 45-year-old Marion Nasskau, died of her injuries at Bromley and District Hospital the following day. Dozens more were injured in the blast; sixty-five people were removed to local hospitals, whilst a further thirty-four needed first-aid treatment.[9] The devastation from the explosion extended over a radius of more than 300 yards. It was the worst loss of life in a V2 incident so far experienced.

Mobile launchers

At the very start of the rocket campaign it was apparent to all that Dornberger's dream had come true. The A4 rocket, as we have seen here, could be successfully delivered to London. But so much time had been lost in the early years through Hitler's indifference to the project and from the devastating *Hydra* raid on Peenemünde that the ambitious plans for a massive onslaught again the UK were no longer possible. Those plans had envisaged a front extending from Cap Gris-Nez to the Cotentin Peninsula. In the giant bunkers at Wizernes and Sottevast, as well as forty-five unprotected smaller sites, the rockets would be fuelled-up and launched against not just London but also Bristol, Southampton and Portsmouth. But all those sites had either been smashed into pieces by the Allied bombers or seized by the liberating armies.

Therefore, that very first V2 to hit the UK, as well as many others that followed, was fired not from France but from Wassenaar, a district of The Hague in Holland. More telling was ▶

undressing for bed: 'Suddenly the ceiling of my bedroom fell on top of me, before I had heard a very big bang. I somehow managed to get downstairs – the top of our house had completely gone. Our family got out of the house to see a sight of complete carnage. The 94 bus, which terminated in our road, had no wheels, and there were bodies lying all over the road.' The roof of the bus had been blown off, landing in another street altogether.

Launched just six minutes earlier, the V2 had directly impacted on the Crooked Billet. William Jessop lived at 3 Parkfield Way, which was less than 100 yards from the back of the pub: 'During the evening of Sunday 19 November 1944, we could hear the dance band music from the Billet

> *"The stairs came adrift, the pipes came out of the walls, the roof came off … After the blast there was a deadly silence and then the screams began."*

going, doors going, front and bathroom … The stairs came adrift, the pipes came out of the walls, the roof came off … After the blast there was a deadly silence and then the screams began.'

Ray Holledge, a 14-year-old-schoolboy at the time, was actually in the saloon bar of the Crooked Billet saying goodnight to his parents and other relatives when the rocket struck. 'We had been celebrating my mother's 57th birthday,' he recalled. 'I was about to leave to keep a date at the Bromley County Club in Crown Lane. Having reached the front corner entrance to the bar I had been called back as I'd forgotten my gloves. The centre of the rocket crater was in fact at this corner of the building. My mother, Eleanor Holledge, was killed and everyone else in our party badly

LEFT AND RIGHT *The scene of devastation that followed the fall of another V2 on 8 March 1945. The V2 in this instance struck Smithfield Market, hitting a building at the junction of Charterhouse Street with Farringdon Road, at 11.30 hours. A total of 110 people were killed.* (HISTORIC MILITARY PRESS)

CENTRE LEFT AND BELOW LEFT
This open area off Tottenham Court Road in London was part of the grounds of Whitefield's Tabernacle. On 25 March 1945, the Tabernacle was destroyed by one of the last V2s to fall on the capital. The replacement structure, built in 1957, is out of view to the right, whilst part of the bomb site, with this damaged grave marker left in situ, became the public space seen here. The V2, Big Ben incident No.1098, impacted at 22.33 hours and left nine dead and thirty-six seriously injured. (COURTESY OF ROBERT MITCHELL)

RIGHT *It has been estimated that during the V1 and V2 offensive some 30,000 homes were totally destroyed and a further 1,250,000 damaged, the majority within the Greater London area. As part of the huge effort to deal with the effects of the V2s, a force of 600 Royal Navy personnel was drafted into London to make 'homes comfortable for the winter ahead'.* (HISTORIC MILITARY PRESS)

NOTES

1. Reported in *The Times*, 8 September 1944.
2. R.V. Jones, *Most Secret War* (Hamish Hamilton, London, 1978), p.459.
3. Ian Jones MBE, *London: Bombed, Blitzed and Blown Up* (Frontline Books, Barnsley, 2016), pp.287-8.
4. ibid, p.289.
5. Quoted in Peter Haining, *The Flying Bomb War* (Robson Books, London, 2002), p.163.
6. Felicity Goodall, *Voices From the Home Front* (David & Charles, London, 2004), p.293.
7. Quoted in Norman Longmate, *Hitler's Rockets* (Frontline Books, Barnsley, 2009), p.341.
8. The accounts of the Bickley incident are all quoted from Jennie Randall's excellent investigation, *Not Forgotten: The Crooked Billet* (The Friend of Jubilee Country Park, Farnborough).
9. Lewis Blake, *Bromley in the Front-Line* (Self-published, Bromley, 1980), p.86.

the fact that it was not launched from some vast elaborate concrete structure, but from a mobile launcher. Each unit consisted of three launchers-cum-transporters called Meillerwagen, each of which carried one rocket and was drawn by a half-track truck which also carried the crew.

The rest of the mobile unit included three tankers transporting the liquid oxygen and alcohol fuels, an armoured command vehicle and a number of staff cars. On reaching the launch site, it took the crew only approximately fifteen minutes to unhitch the Meillerwagen and place it in a vertical position on stabilizers. The rocket was then fuelled-up and the final pre-launch checks carried out. In little more than an hour after arriving at the launch site, the rocket was ready to be ignited.

Such was the thrust delivered by the engine, all the fuel was consumed in just fifty-four seconds, but by then the rocket had reached a speed of nearly 2,000 miles an hour. The rocket reached a height of between fifty and sixty miles above the earth.

Five minutes after launch the rocket impacted having plunged to the ground at a speed of up to 2,500 miles per hour. Dealing with such a threat, however, proved almost impossible. ●

Operation Big Ben

IT WAS OBVIOUSLY UNREALISTIC TO EXPECT HEAVY BOMBERS TO FIND AND ATTACK SUCH SMALL, SHIFTING TARGETS AS THE MOBILE V2 LAUNCH UNITS. IT WAS TO THE ALLIED FIGHTER PILOTS THAT THE AUTHORITIES TURNED.

Having considered the various options, the task of countering the mobile V2 launch sites was handed, in great part, to the fighters, more specifically the Typhoons, Tempests and clipped-wing Spitfire Mark XVIs of Nos. 124, 303, 451, 453, 602 and 229/603 squadrons, which were to act in a dive-bombing role. This became known as Operation *Big Ben*.

BELOW *A V2 being raised on its Meillerwagen in preparation for firing.* (NARA)

Though the V2 sites were mobile, there were a number of areas where it was believed that the rockets would be launched from, and the *Big Ben* sorties were not just speculative but were directed to a particular point. The rocket firing companies needed an infrastructure of transport and ▶

storage facilities, with the rockets being moved from the factories by rail and road and then stored within easy reach of the potential launch areas. It had been found that the longer the completed rockets were left in storage before use, the greater the chance of components failing. So, the aim was to get them to the firing troops and then launch them as quickly as possible. The Hague, it was found, had an excellent road and rail infrastructure as well as wooded areas from where the mobile units could operate hidden by trees.

Resistance groups in Holland were able to supply information regarding the launch sites, which enabled the fighter squadrons to direct their attacks at those points. It was learned that the Germans had made preparations to store rockets on three properties situated at Wassenaar, just outside The

ABOVE *The white stream of a V2 rocket trail photographed early in the morning, over the border area between Holland and Germany, during December 1944.* (HISTORIC MILITARY PRESS)

BELOW RIGHT

A Meillerwagen with its V2 raised. At the launch site, crews raised the rocket vertically with the Meillerwagen, then fuelled it with alcohol and liquid oxygen. After several tests and adjustments, the rocket could be fired from the safety of an armoured control car nearby. (NARA)

Hague, and which were named respectively Terhorst, Eikenhorst, and Raaphorst. At the first two there were comparatively small wooded areas, which for various reasons seemed eminently suitable for the purpose; Raaphorst was a rather extensive property, and the intelligence reports did not give more precise information.

Standing patrols of four Spitfires were flown throughout the hours of daylight over these suspected areas, hoping for a sign of suspicious activity. One squadron would always be held in readiness in case a report was received of preparations being made for a launch.

During the first ten days of the rocket campaign, RAF fighters mounted approximately 1,000 sorties against suspected V2 locations. They attacked a variety of targets, including road, rail, and water transport vehicles and installations, suspicious constructions, and German troops. It was difficult to assess the effectiveness of such attacks, but on one occasion when Tempests attacked a suspected firing point an explosion occurred that was so violent as to wreck the leading aircraft. Afterwards a large, shallow crater was seen, such as might have been caused by the detonation of a rocket in the firing position.

Despite concerns, Bomber Command was also given Terhorst and Eikenhorst as targets, these being added to the list of *Crossbow* operations. Consequently, on 17 September a small force dropped 172 tons of bombs on Eikenhorst. It was later discovered, however, that this was not a V2 storage facility.

Fears that the Allies were about to cross the Rhine into Germany in Operation *Market Garden* and thus cut off Holland from the Reich, saw the launching teams being moved to Doedrecht and the Burgsteinfurt-Münster-Coesfeld region, with the new target area for the rockets being Allied bases in Belgian, in addition to the northern French industrial areas. As is well-known, the bridge

over the Lower Rhine at Arnhem proved to be a bridge too far and one of the launching teams, Batterie 444, returned to Holland a week later. It was on 25 September that the rockets began to fall once again on the UK.

Creating disorder and panic

At 19.10 hours that day in late September a rocket fired by Batterie 444 fell near Diss in Suffolk. Further rockets landed in East Anglia over the course of the following days, and then, on 3 October, London once again became a target. Great difficulty was experienced locating where these attacks came from, though the area around The Hague again appeared to be the most likely. On 15 October, Fighter Command was re-born after being disbanded in 1943. Roderick Hill continued to lead Fighter Command and be responsible for eliminating the V2 threat. To avoid civilian casualties, Hill drew up a list of targets which were at least 250 yards from the nearest houses and from 21 November the *Big Ben* operations began in earnest.

Squadron Leader Ernest Esau DFC, of 453 Squadron RAAF, gave a talk on the BBC about these missions against the V2s: 'To see the trail when a rocket went up was an amazing sight. I've seen several as I was approaching the Dutch coast. I first noticed a trail starting at about 8,000 feet, a practically vertical trail – it soared right up to a

fantastic height, and it grew at an incredible speed and then it gradually leaned over towards England.

'Sometimes I saw the rocket itself. It looked rather like a small

black speck; there was no flame about it, or if there was, I couldn't see it in the daytime. It was such a tiny black speck, but it left behind a fantastically broad white fluffy trail, and that gradually dispersed with the wind, and disappeared …

'It was quite obvious that the only thing the air force could do against such a weapon was to prevent it from being fired – the rocket bomb couldn't be intercepted in the air as the flying bomb had been, by fighters, flak and balloons. So Bomber Command attacked the places where rockets and rocket fuel were manufactured; [the] Tactical Air Force attacked transport to prevent them being brought up

> *"It was quite obvious that the only thing the air force could do against such a weapon was to prevent it from being fired …"*

to the firing points; and towards the end, squadrons of Fighter Command joined in with TAF [2nd Tactical Air Force], but at first Fighter Command

concentrated on attacking the sites to prevent the Germans establishing any fixed programme of operating.

'The sites were very small and extremely mobile, so we kept up continuous patrols during the hours of daylight. We aimed to create such disorder and panic that no permanent firing site could be established, no regular supplies delivered, no regular firing programme followed. But ▶

RIGHT AND CENTRE RIGHT *These two pictures depict parts of a supply train full of V2s that was halted, through a mixture of air and ground attack, near the small town of Bromskirchen in Germany. The train, which had been en route to The Netherlands, was divided by its crew in an effort to escape, though both halves were subsequently captured by troops of the American 3rd Armored Division on 29 March 1945. The train yielded a haul of complete rockets, a number of warheads as well carriages full of parts such as carbon-graphite V2 rudders, fuzes, and batteries.* (SAN DIEGO AIR & SPACE MUSEUM)

CENTRE LEFT *Squadron Leader Ernest Esau DFC, Officer Commanding 453 Squadron RAAF, pictured whilst 453 Squadron RAAF, which 'has been engaged in the attacks on V2 sites', was based at RAF Swannington. Esau concluded his BBC broadcast by stating that 'in the five months the V2s held our interest, the squadron did over 1,000 sorties. March was the biggest month – March was a terrific month – flying conditions were good and the ground crew worked flat out.'* (AUSTRALIAN WAR MEMORIAL; UK2201)

it wasn't a case of having a certain number of sites to eliminate and the job was finished, they were so mobile that they sprung up unobtrusively like mushrooms overnight.

'The sites were centred round The Hague – [the] capital of Holland. This city is surrounded by large woods; they give excellent cover and the Germans made use of them to camouflage their activities. Every site was camouflaged – none of us ever saw one, but we were so carefully briefed that we could pinpoint the target easily, on the basis of photo-reconnaissance and other information …

'Every attack we made was different, of course, but the general procedure was always the same. Before we left base, we were very carefully briefed for a particular target, and when we'd finished our general reconnaissance of the area we checked up on our information about the target.

'Then the leader got ready for his bombing run, and began to talk up, giving the approximate time when he was coming down – and the time gradually worked down to about a thirty-second warning, and the last order was "Going down now". Then everybody peeled off after him in a very steep power dive form 9,000 feet down to 3,000. We got a good view of the target in that dive and were able to aim our bombs.

'Everyone followed the leader in and attacked in rapid succession, and then we'd use the tremendous speed gained in the dive to zoom climb and to gain height. The pull-out followed by the vertical climb usually resulted in blackout lasting ten to fifteen seconds – during that time the aircraft flew itself, but I always felt quite normal when I came to, and I

never heard anyone complain …

'The whole rocket site area was always under an alert when we went there, so we never saw any life there at all, and that was terribly depressing. All the streets were bare; it looked as though no one had lived there for hundreds of years. It was very seldom that we saw even an odd car or transport. In other places there was quite a bit of traffic, and some shipping, but here, nothing at all. There was nothing on the water either, not even a rowing boat.

'Up north of The Hague there's still a large building with the usual very big circle with a Red Cross in the middle, the international marking for a hospital. The Germans used the woods adjoining this building as a rocket site, so we were faced with a

> *"This weapon is another attempt by the enemy to attack the morale of our civil population in the vain hope that he may somehow by this means stave off the defeat which faces him in the field."*

problem of hitting the site without hitting the hospital. We attacked the site several times with good results, the majority of bombs falling in exactly the right place, with no damage to the hospital.

'Another place they used to fire rockets from was a long wood almost in the centre of town – it's probably a public garden. There was a canal running across it and several roads through it. The problem here was to plaster the wood without doing any damage to the built-up area around. There are some film studios in The Hague, very large film studios. The Germans were storing stuff in there – liquid oxygen – and filling up some V-2s. So, we attacked it with a dozen aircraft and burnt it to the ground; we hit it at eleven in the morning, and it was still burning at seven that night.'[1]

All is revealed

Meanwhile, on 10 November 1944, the Prime Minister officially told the nation what the general public had suspected for weeks. 'Last February I told Parliament that the Germans were preparing to attack this country by means of long-range rockets,' Churchill declared, 'and I referred again to the possibility of this form of attack in my statement in this House on 6th July.

'For the last few weeks the enemy has been using its new weapon, the long-range rocket, and a number have landed at widely scattered points in this country. In all, the casualties and damage have so far not been heavy, though I am sure the House would wish me to express our sympathy with the victims of this as of other attacks. No official statement about the attack has hitherto been issued. The reason for this silence was that any announcement might have given information useful to the enemy, and we were confirmed in this course by the fact that, until two days ago, the enemy had made no mention of this weapon in his communiques.

'Last Wednesday an official announcement, followed by a number of highly coloured accounts of the attacks on this country, was issued by the German High Command. I do not propose to comment upon it except to say that the statements in this announcement are a good reflection of what the German Government would wish their people to believe, and of

ABOVE LEFT A surviving, restored V2 and Meillerwagen that can be seen at the National Museum of the US Air Force in Dayton, Ohio. Both rocket and trailer had previously been displayed in the open at the Aberdeen Proving Grounds in Maryland. (NATIONAL MUSEUM OF THE US AIR FORCE)

ABOVE RIGHT A Spitfire XVI taxying. Of the Spitfire, Squadron Leader Ernest Esau stated in his broadcast that it was 'the finest all-round performer we have produced – the Mosquito boys wouldn't agree with that but still'. (COURTESY OF THE LATE DR ALFRED PRICE)

BELOW Spitfire XVIs of 453 Squadron at RAF Hawkinge in May 1945 soon after its attacks against V2 sites had ended. (COURTESY OF JOHN BENNETT, VIA ANDREW THOMAS)

their desperate need to afford them some encouragement.

'I may, however, mention a few facts. The rocket contains approximately the same quantity of high explosive as the flying bomb. However, it is designed to penetrate rather deeper before exploding. This results in somewhat heavier damage in the immediate vicinity of the crater, but rather less extensive blast effect around. The rocket flies through the stratosphere, going up to 60 or 70 miles, and outstrips sound. Because of its high speed, no reliable or sufficient public warning can, in present circumstances, be given.

'There is, however, no need to exaggerate the danger. The scale and effects of the attack have not hitherto been significant. Some rockets have been fired at us from the island of Walcheren. This is now in our hands, and other areas from which rockets have, or can at present be fired against this country will, doubtless, be over-run by our Forces in due course. We cannot, however, be certain that the enemy will not be able to increase the range, either by reducing the weight of the war-head or by other methods. Nor, on the other hand, can we be certain that any new launching areas which he may establish further back will not, also, in turn, be over-run by the advancing Allied Armies.

'The use of this weapon is another attempt by the enemy to attack the morale of our civil population in the vain hope that he may

somehow by this means stave off the defeat which faces him in the field. Doubtless the enemy has hoped by his announcement to induce us to give him information which he has failed to get otherwise. I am sure that this House, the Press and the public will refuse to oblige him in this respect.'[2]

Dive-bombing Spitfies

Operations by the fighters continued throughout the rest of 1944, weather permitting. Altogether, between 21 November and the end of the year Hill's men undertook 470 fighter-bomber sorties against rocket targets and dropped fifty-four tons of bombs in the course of them. In these operations no effort was spared to ensure that the bombs were dropped with precision. A characteristic attack delivered during this phase was one made by Nos. 229, 453, and 602 squadrons on Christmas Eve. The target was a block of flats near the centre of The Hague, which the Germans were using to house the firing troops in that district. The building was so badly damaged that the Germans had to abandon it.

The dangers of the low-level bombing undertaken by the fighters can be seen in one such attack, on 11 December, which was detailed in the Operations Record Book of 229 Squadron. This was the third armed reconnaissance of the day, the sortie being led by Flight Lieutenant Patterson. The flight took off from RAF Coltishall ▶

at 15.00 hours with Wassenaar en Vreugd as the target: 'Crossing near Westhoofd at 11,000 feet they flew to the target to find it obscured in mist. They orbited at 10,000 feet waiting for the mist to clear and then "peeled off" in a steep turn to dive from more or less E. to W. from 10,000 feet to 4,000 feet. F/Lt. Patterson's bombs fell about 5 yards from the corner of a very tall and large 5 storey building about 100 yards North of the suspected site. All the rest fell on the pinpoint which was North of and along the side of the road.

'They were met by the heaviest flak yet, a very intense carpet of light flak, very accurate and from the woods about 1 mile round the pinpoint. It burst in white puffs and P/O Doidge thought it was mist. F/Lt. McAndrew fired into it and F/Sgt. O'Reilly, flying No.4 had to decide whether to dive straight in against what looked [like] hopeless odds, or pull away. He did the former and dived straight into it. Nobody was hit although they were still followed by heavy accurate flak and light flak from the coast off Hague and Katwijk.'[3]

As a result of the dive-bombing, the scale of the attack upon London declined from an average of nearly seven rockets a day at the end of November, to four a day in the middle of December, and then three-and-a-half at the end of the month. Moreover, the Germans took to carrying out most of the firing at night, and the apparent accuracy of the shooting decreased. It must be admitted that as well as the daring efforts of the Allied pilots, another reason for the limited scale of the rocket attack was almost certainly the armed reconnaissance and rail

RIGHT *One that did not reach its target. A section of a V2 is examined by a Dutch Army bomb disposal officer following its recovery from its crash site in Rotterdam Port, Holland, on 15 July 1964.* (DUTCH NATIONAL ARCHIVES)

BELOW *Standing in the cockpit of his aircraft is Wing Commander Donald George Andrews DFC, the leader of the first Australian fighter Wing to operate in Europe. This was a Spitfire wing which included the RAAF's Nos. 451 and 453 squadrons. It was devoted entirely to countermeasures against the V2. Operating from bases in Britain and on the Continent, the wing flew 1,328 sorties over Holland, bombing and strafing launching sites, workshops and transport, and cutting railway lines leading to the firing sites. Note the nose art and letters 'DGA'.* (AUSTRALIAN WAR MEMORIAL; UK2743)

interdiction sorties flown by the 2nd Tactical Air Force (which had been added to Roderick Hill's command to assist with *Big Ben*) over the enemy's lines of communication. This restricted the rate at which the rockets were transported to the launching sites.

Then in the New Year the scale of attack went up again. During the first half of January 1945 an average of more than eight rockets a day reached the UK. Thereafter the rate of fire declined a little, only to rise again early in February, until an average of ten rockets a day was attained in the middle of the month. Moreover, the Germans again took to doing more than half their firing in daylight, and their accuracy

improved. In an average week in January and the first half of February 1945, twice as many people were killed or seriously injured by rockets as in a corresponding period in December. Clearly, the fighter-bomber programme was not such an effective deterrent as had been thought. Something more was needed.

Dutch Disaster

If it was proving difficult to target the mobile launch sites, the solution was to attack the static sites – the centres of manufacture, especially those that produced the liquid oxygen. From intelligence provided by the likes of SOE, it was believed that there were eight factories in Holland associated with the rocket programme. These included one at Alblasserdam, near Dordrecht, which was successfully

attacked by the 2nd Tactical Air Force on 22 January. Another, at Ijmuiden, consisted of two buildings so closely surrounded by other factories that the prospect of a successful attack was remote. The third, at Loosduinen, on the outskirts of The Hague, was adjoined on three sides by Dutch civilian property. Despite the risks, this was targeted for the first time on 3 February, the pilots attacking from the direction in which there were no houses adjoining the factory. Four further attacks were made until the site was considered to have been demolished beyond further use by the enemy.

While extreme care had been taken not to damage Dutch civilian property, this was not always the case. In one tragic incident on 3 March, a mixed force of light and medium bombers of the 2nd Tactical Air Force, aiming for a known V2 site at Haagse Bos, dropped bombs very wide of the target and many fell in the Bezuidenhout neighbourhood of The Hague, killing 511 civilians.[4]

Warrant Officer Max Baerlein, on patrol in his 602 Squadron Spitfire, flew over Bezuidenhout that same day after the attack, which had taken place between 08.00 hours and 09.00 hours: 'We were not in the area when the bombing took place but the whole place was a mass of flames and the bombers had gone. The significance was very obvious to us as on the bombing runs we had made, up until then, we had always taken great care not to touch any civilian buildings in the area, only releasing our bombs at the lowest altitude that would enable us to pull out of the dive. The mess we saw from the air was, in consequence, most distressing. We were shocked to see that all the efforts we had made to avoid civilian houses had been to no avail.'[5]

After the disaster at Bezuidenhout the decision was taken to cease attacks against targets in The Hague and a proposal was put forward to try and bring down the rockets by anti-aircraft fire. General Pile asked for an

operational trial of a scheme designed to ensure that the rockets would pass through a curtain of shell-fragments as they approached the earth. The scientists, however, objected on the grounds that the amount of shells that would have to be put up to create such a wall of fire would be just as dangerous and alarming as the rocket itself. Though the scheme was not completely dismissed, the war in Europe was brought to a conclusion before a trial could take place. ●

NOTES

1 Squadron Leader Ernest Esau's account was first broadcast on Thursday, 16 April 1945.
2 Hansard, House of Commons debate, 10 November 1944, vol 404 cc1653-4.
3 Quoted in Bill Simpson *Spitfire Dive-Bombers Versus the V2* (Pen & Sword, Barnsley, 2007), pp.121-2.
4 A further 344 people were wounded, whilst 20,000 were rendered homeless. A total of 3,250 houses were destroyed, and a further 3,241 damaged to various degrees – of which 391 had to be demolished. Five churches and nine schools were destroyed.
5 Bill Simpson, pp.170-1.

The Nazi Supergun

THE FLYING BOMB AND THE A4 ROCKET WERE NOT THE ONLY SECRET WEAPONS BUILT BY THE GERMANS DURING THE SECOND WORLD WAR.

T he success of Operation *Hydra* had demonstrated just how exposed and vulnerable the V1 and V2 weapons programmes were. But these were not the only secret weapons being developed at that time by the Germans and after the virtual destruction of the facilities at Peenemünde, Hitler urged every effort to be made to speed up the development of the weapon that would be the V3 – often referred to by its codename of *Hochdruckpumpe*, or 'High Pressure Pump'.

This project had first been mentioned to Hitler by Speer in May 1943 but after *Hydra* the Führer agreed to Speer's suggestion that development of the weapon should go ahead without further testing: 'Risks must be stood to award contract at once,' the Führer is reported to have told Speer. The V3 took the form of a very long gun which would fire projectiles a great distance at a very high rate of fire. It differed from conventional guns in that its projectile was propelled not by a single charge but by a number of charges along the length of the gun barrel which progressively increased the velocity of the projectile. It was also smooth-bored which meant that it would not suffer the degradation that affected rifled weapons. Instead, the required spin on the projectile to give it stability in flight was achieved by small fins on the body of the projectile which opened when the projectile was shot into the air.

Tests on the *Hochdruckpumpe* had already taken place earlier in 1943 at the Hillersleben artillery range some fifteen miles north-

west of Magdeburg. While the tests demonstrated that the principle behind the idea worked, the muzzle velocity was far below expectations which meant the projectiles were not discharged with sufficient speed to reach the kind of distances that would be necessary to bombard London. A velocity of 5,000 feet per second was considered necessary, but only 3,300 feet per second was attained. Even so, this was enough to fire the projectiles an impressive distance of fifty-eight miles. It was believed that more chambers along the length of the barrel would resolve this, with as many as twenty-eight being proposed.

The weapon could be concealed far more easily than a complex rocket site and Hitler's imagination was further fired by the proposal to site fifty of these guns in the Pas-de-Calais which would each fire chrome nickel steel, 9 feet long, dart-like 140kg shells carrying a 55lb explosive charge at London at the rate of up to 600 an hour – all of which, it was hoped, would completely flatten the British capital. The man who had explained the theory behind the V3 to Speer, August Cönders, chief engineer of the Röchling Stahlwerk AG company, was duly given approval to produce a full-size prototype. An artillery battalion was also formed to fire the guns and, by the end of 1943, the crews were undergoing training.

Highly secret though the *Hochdruckpumpe* was, activity related to this supergun had not gone unnoticed by the staff of the CIU. In September 1943 photographs had been taken by PRU pilots of work being undertaken near the hamlet of Mimoyecques in the Pas-de-Calais about twelve miles from Boulogne, and just ninety-five miles from central London. Though unaware of the nature or purpose of the site, despite descriptions being received from the French resistance of giant 'mortars' dug into the ground, it did not become a target for Allied bombers until November 1943 when it was attacked by aircraft of the US Ninth Air Force.

Bringing Britain to her knees

The true nature of the Mimoyecques site, originally codenamed *Wiese* ('Meadow') or *Bauvorhaben 711* ('Construction Project 711') by the Germans, was only discovered when it was

RIGHT *Pictured after the capture of the Mimoyecques site, this is one of the exit chambers for the barrels set in a concrete slab up on the plateau above the tunnel. This chamber, or aperture, was to have been protected by a large steel plate - see page 103.* (HISTORIC MILITARY PRESS)

BELOW *Pictured from just inside its entrance, the main railway tunnel of the eastern site of the Mimoyecques V3 complex stretches away into the distance for a total of about 630 metres. One of the eleven cross galleries (numbered 3 to 13 by the Germans), can be seen on the left, these in turn being driven at right angles to the main tunnel at regular intervals.* (HISTORIC MILITARY PRESS)

captured by Allied ground forces, in the form of the Canadian 3rd Infantry Division, on 5 September 1944. This was revealed to the general public in newspaper reports by Douglas Williams, a correspondent for the *Daily Telegraph* and *The Scotsman*, under the headline: 'Secrets of V3, Giant Cannon Designed to Wipe out London'. Reporting from Mimoyecques, Williams wrote: 'Amid desolate chalk hills, six miles from the channel coast, in an area thickly pitted with yawning bomb holes, I have visited the site of Germany's third secret weapon, the V3. With this the enemy had planned to fire a continuous barrage of rocket shells from giant cannon into London …

'The site was designed to accommodate 50 400-feet long gun tubes, sunk to a depth of 350 feet below the ground, and protected by a solid 18 feet thick concrete apron. It is estimated that the monster weapons would have had a combined rate of fire of at least 10 rounds a minute, the shells landing in the heart of London, 95 miles away across the Channel …

> *"Apparently it was hoped that, with the Civil Defence services already fully occupied with V bombs and ordinary rockets, they would create such havoc as to compel the evacuation of London…"*

'Apparently it was hoped that, with the Civil Defence services already fully occupied with V bombs and ordinary rockets, they would create such havoc as to compel the evacuation of London, with all the administrative complications and damage to British morale that such a step would have involved … Once the site had been finished, the thickness of its concrete cover and the depth at which the pieces were embedded, would have made it invulnerable to any air attack, no matter how heavy the bombs employed …

'Thousands of workmen, all slave press-gangs of the Todt organisation, laboured day and night for nearly a year. The stage of completion, despite the heavy bombing, to which the work had been advanced, pays tribute to the enemy's determination to try at all costs to finish what was obviously a job of the highest order of priority.

'No trace had been found either of guns or ammunition. I am informed that some were actually delivered on the site, but they were apparently removed by the Germans when they left, either because they desired to ▶

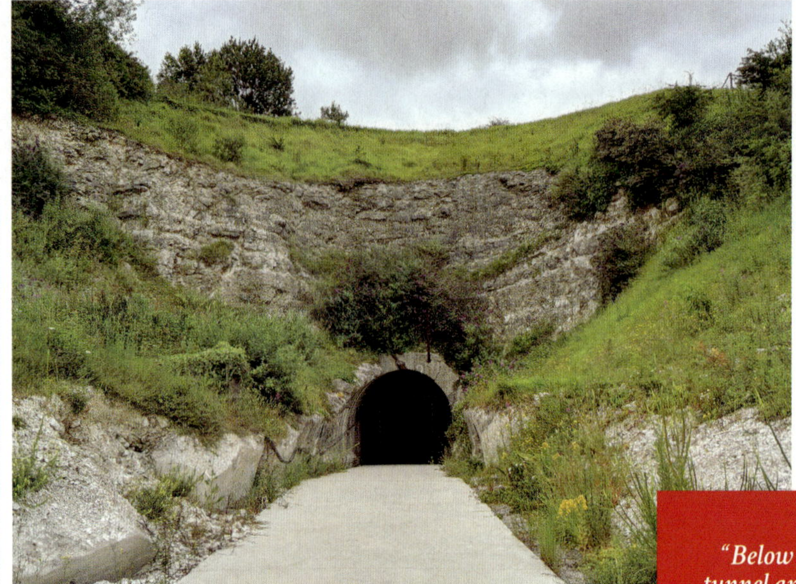

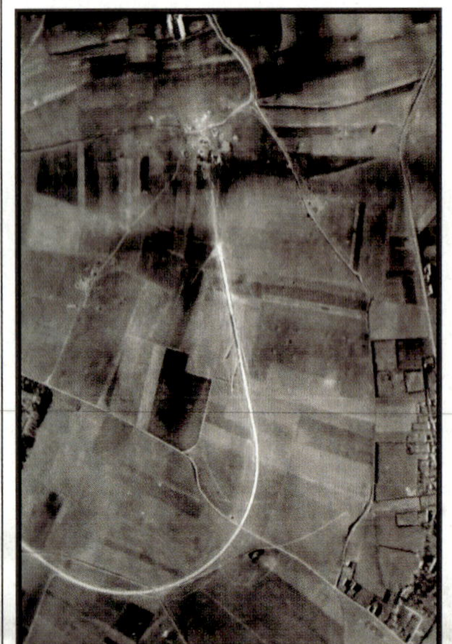

RIGHT *The entrance to the railway tunnel at the eastern site at Mimoyecques as it appears today. The site is a museum, having reopened to the public in its current form on 1 July 2010.* (HISTORIC MILITARY PRESS)

RIGHT *Taken on 3 November 1943, this aerial reconnaissance photograph clearly shows the newly laid railway line which sweeps round in a large curve before heading underground towards the top of the image.* (HISTORIC MILITARY PRESS)

conceal the secret of the new weapon or possibly because they hoped to use them later at another site.

'The guns were set in deep inclined shafts, at an angle of about 55 degrees, rising from the crescent-shaped chalk hill west of the main Boulogne – Calais road. A standard gauge railway, completed but never used, leads to the site. it disappears into a vault-like tunnel of solid concrete, of impressive proportions, some 700 yards long and 30 feet high by 25 feet broad. An unloading platform giving access to chambers and galleries, opening off the tunnel into the hillside, runs its entire length.

'Below this main tunnel are two other smaller tunnels. The entire workings are buried underground, some penetrating to about 350 feet. Superimposed over all, covering an area of several acres, is a slab of concrete up to 18 feet thick in places, with a number of square exits.

"Below this main tunnel are two other smaller tunnels. The entire workings are buried underground, some penetrating to about 350 feet"

'At the entrance to the tunnel is a concrete building housing a large electric generator, to produce the 4000 kilowatts of power that the enemy would need to operate this colossal engine of destruction. In the huge dump of steel girders and unassembled spare parts that were abandoned in the hurry of departure around the workings was found technical machinery, indicating the intention to construct a complicated lift system, presumably to handle the ammunition.

'To-day the Mimoyecques site is an abandoned wilderness, devastated and churned up by heavy bombs, with craters 30 to 50 feet deep. Here and there emerge broken slabs of concrete and portions of huge timbers tossed into the air. But less than a year ago the area was a teeming anthill of action as German engineers pitilessly drove their conscript labour to complete the last refinement in secret weapons, which they hoped would finally bring Britain to her knees.'[1]

BELOW *A Handley Page Halifax pictured over the V3 site at Mimoyecques during Bomber Command's daylight attack on 6 July 1944.* (HISTORIC MILITARY PRESS)

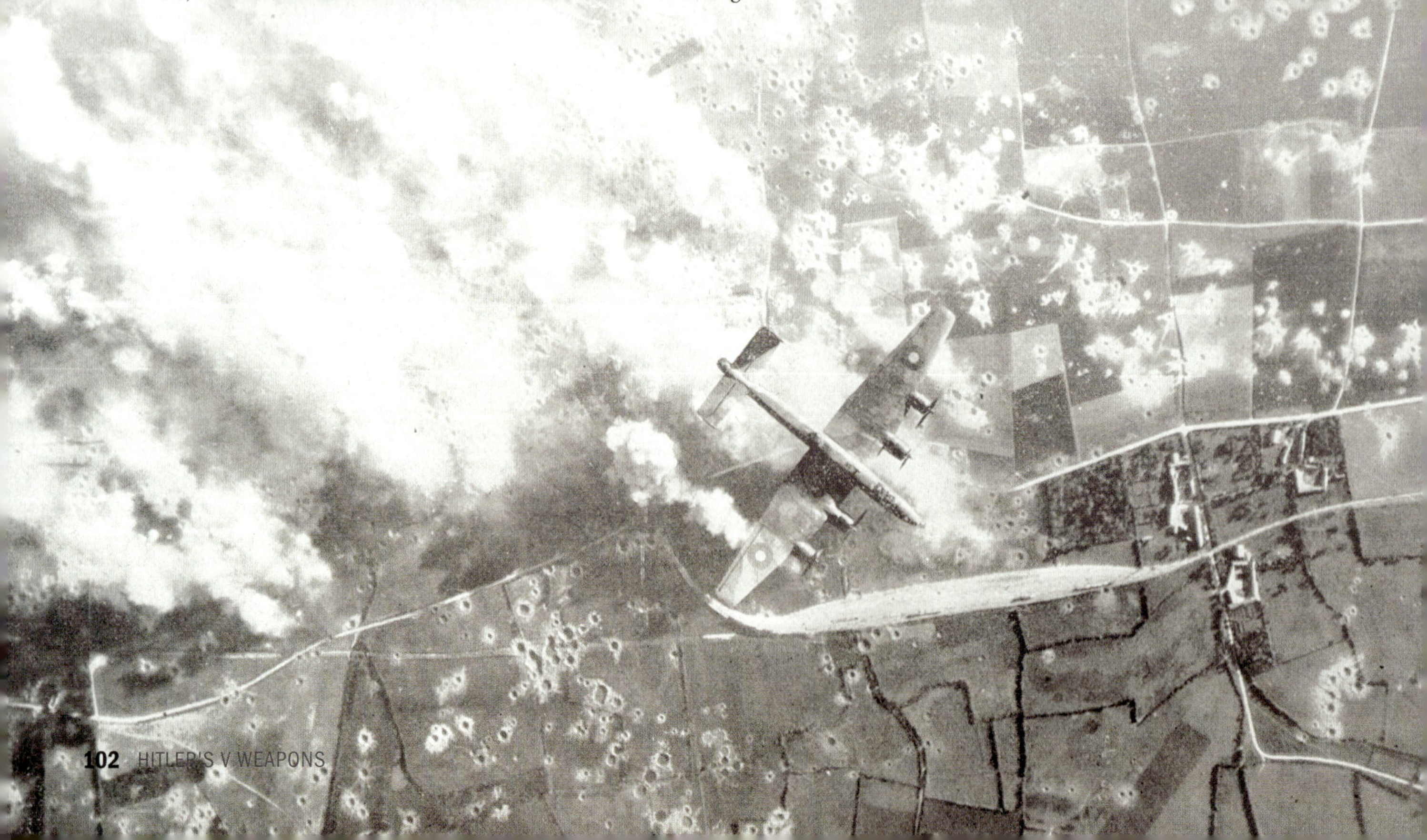

Turning to the Tallboys

The Mimoyecques site had, as Douglas Williams described, been severely damaged by Allied bombers since that first raid in November which, on the 5th of that month, saw seventy-one B-26 Martin Marauders and 48 Consolidated B-24 Liberators deliver 360 tons of bombs on the site. But poor visibility resulted in inaccurate bombing, with some bombers aborting their attacks. Three days later, Mimoyecques was the target of seventy-two Douglas Bostons of the RAF's Second Tactical Air Force with reportedly slightly better results.

Now aware that the site had been spotted by the Allies, the Germans knew that the RAF and USAAF would continue to return until the place was blasted into oblivion. So the western of the two batteries was abandoned with debris left unmoved to deceive the Allies while continuing to work surreptitiously on the eastern battery. Consequently, no further raids were undertaken until March 1944

ABOVE *This surviving example of the large steel plates that protected the openings in the concrete slabs up on the Mimoyecques plateau can be seen near the visitor centre at the museum. Weighing some sixty tons apiece, each of the steel plates has five apertures for the five barrels of each V3 cluster.* (HISTORIC MILITARY PRESS)

when, after receiving information from the French Resistance that Mimoyecques was still an active site, the place was attacked twice. This was followed by four attacks in April, three in May and two more in June. Despite the intensity of the attacks, the construction of the site deep in the hillside meant that damage had not been such as to prevent work continuing on the eastern site.

On 5 July 1944, a British intelligence report confirmed the presence of three openings on the surface of the Mimoyecques plateau. These apertures, the report added, were directed precisely at the centre of London. It was also noted that one of the openings contained an object that was identified as being the barrel

of a mortar gun, indicating that the installation of the site's armament had begun.[2] The importance of neutralising the Mimoyecques facility had suddenly intensified, and the RAF response was immediate and spectacular.

The very next morning, a force of 100 Halifax bombers was despatched to Mimoyecques to carry out a traditional 'carpet-bombing' raid, in the course of which a total of 464 2,000lb bombs were dropped. It was a few hours later that the decisive strike was made, the raiders this time being sixteen Lancasters from 617 Squadron, each carrying a Tallboy. Led by Group Captain Leonard Cheshire, who shortly afterwards was awarded the Victoria Cross, the Dambusters' Lancasters took to the air a little after 13.30 hours on 6 July 1944. With Cheshire out in front at the controls of a Mustang III and Flight Lieutenant Fawke in a de Havilland Mosquito to act as target markers, the Mimoyecques site initially proved difficult to identify due to the enormous amount of damage in the area from the previous bombing raids.

'Cheshire marked the target from 800 feet in a dive attack,' notes one account. 'Although dropped on target they failed to show up at all well in daylight, but Munro led in the bombers as the sky became a nightmare of flak. Flying Officer Ian Ross's machine was hit and so was Stanford's. Flying Officer Lee had all four engines hit and three of his crew wounded from shell splinters and ▶

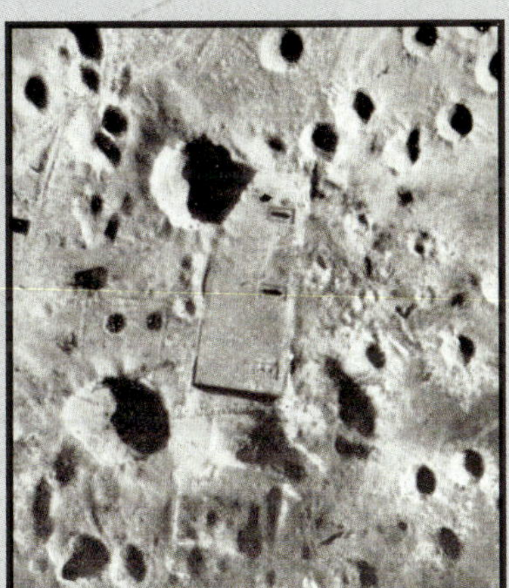

LEFT *A vertical aerial reconnaissance photograph of part of the Mimoyecques plateau taken after Bomber Command's daylight attack on 6 July 1944. It shows one of the concrete slabs that would have housed the steel plates that protected the clusters of five V3 barrels. The larger craters are the result of Tallboy bombs.* (HISTORIC MILITARY PRESS)

Churchill Orders Mimoyecques' Destruction

No sooner had the Mimoyecques complex been captured, it became, understandably, the subject of much interest by Allied scientists and weapons experts. Among those who toured the site was Colonel T.R.B. Sanders, who, employed by the Ministry of Supply, led the Sanders Mission, the remit of which was to examine the various V weapon sites in Northern France in 1944.

The tunnels at Mimoyecques were duly explored by Sanders in November and December that year. In his subsequent report, dated 21 February 1945, Sanders made a clear recommendation – the 'destruction of Mimoyecques should be an absolute priority'. Having subsequently reviewed Sanders' report, Churchill concurred and ordered that the V3 installation should be rendered unusable by any other party. Negotiations to this effect between the Foreign Office and the provisional French government ended without agreement, and on 25 April 1945, Churchill decided to 'act first and explain after'.

Specialist teams from the Royal Engineers placed thirty-eight explosive charges, totalling thirty-six tonnes of TNT, in the tunnels, particularly at the thirty-metre level, to deny access to deeper areas, and at the openings on the surface of the Mimoyecques plateau. These charges were detonated on 9 and 14 May 1945, the French only being informed after the event. It is said that such actions infuriated General de Gaulle who considered them 'a violation of France's national sovereignty'. So extensive was the effects of the explosions, that even today large sections of the tunnels remain blocked.

he had to jettison his bomb into the sea. Kell had an engine cut out on his first run but he turned for a second, dropping his bomb from 17,000 feet. Knilans made his run but the bombsight went u/s so he had to abort and head for home. Two other aircraft did not bomb as the crews could not identify the target.

'The main hit, by Flying Officer Nick Ross, fell in the main area of the construction and caused a subsidence over an area of 160 by 120 yards. The roads and railways to the east of the tunnel entrance were completely severed. There was no chance of its being repaired … Several hundred of these workers were known to have been trapped in the tunnel, thinking it the safest place during an air raid.'[3]

At least eight Tallboys hit the target during this attack. The seismic effect of the mighty Tallboys led to the collapse of several arches in the tunnel. The pounding by the Tallboys also led to the gun chambers being blocked with debris and caused some flooding.[4]

With Allied ground troops pushing out from the Normandy beaches, and with little possibility of repairing the damage, the Mimoyecques bunker complex was abandoned – though this was not clear to the Allies at the time (almost all of the forced labour had been moved from the site by 26 July). Consequently, there were three subsequent raids on Mimoyecques and by the end of the bombing campaign, over 4,100 tons of bombs had been dropped, more than on any other V weapons site.

Into the future

Early in the Iran-Iraqi war of the 1980s, Saddam Hussein engaged world-renowned artillery expert Gerald V. Bull, whose lifetime obsession was the construction of

ABOVE *Some of the last attacks on Mimoyecques involved aircraft from operations* Aphrodite *and* Anvil, *these being the codenames given to US schemes to deploy radio-controlled B-17 and PB4Y bombers as precision-guided munitions against bunkers and other hardened/reinforced enemy facilities. The B-17F seen here, nicknamed* The Careful Virgin, *was directed against Mimoyecques on 4 August 1944, this being the first* Aphrodite *strike against this site, but it impacted short of the target due to controller error.* (NATIONAL MUSEUM OF THE US AIR FORCE)

RIGHT *On 12 August 1944, another Operation* Anvil *mission set out to attack Mimoyecques, but the Liberator 'robot' exploded prematurely over the Suffolk coast. Both of the crew, Lieutenant Wilford J. Willy and Lieutenant Joseph P. Kennedy Jr., seen here, were killed in the blast.* (COURTESY OF THE LATE EARL P. OLSEN)

LEFT *Located in one of the side galleries at Mimoyecques, this memorial commemorates three RAF bombers lost during the various attacks on the V3 complex.* (HISTORIC MILITARY PRESS)

MIDDLE LEFT *The memorial to Lieutenant Joseph P. Kennedy Jr that is in a chamber off the main railway tunnel at Mimoyecques.* (HISTORIC MILITARY PRESS)

BELOW LEFT *This stretch of railway tunnel at Mimoyecques is that which is furthest from the visitor entrance. Along the west side is the unloading platform.* (HISTORIC MILITARY PRESS)

BELOW RIGHT *One of the inclines at Mimoyecques which, intended to have housed the V3 gun, still reaches the surface above today.* (HISTORIC MILITARY PRESS)

a 'Supergun' based on many of the fundamentals inherent in the V3. It was intended that the gun would be able to fire artillery shells thousands of miles into enemy territory. Some parts of the gun, codenamed 'Project Babylon', were manufactured in the UK. The project was not completed as the gun was a potential threat to Israel and Bull, a Canadian national, was assassinated, it is presumed, by Mossad.

The Germans on the long-range bombardment programme did not have just three weapons under consideration. Among these were other rocket developments, including the A9, a winged version of the A4. This would be shot into space and upon re-entry would 'bounce' on the earth's atmosphere to send it a greater distance, increasing its range to cover most of England – suggestions being made that it could travel 450 miles which would then mean these rockets could be fired at the UK from deep in Germany.

There were also plans for two-stage rocket, the A10, which would reach the United States – the first intercontinental ballistic missile and the forerunners of the weapons that came to dominate the post-war world. Work on this rocket began in 1940 under Walter Thiel, which would see a pack of A4 engines as the booster rocket which would generate a thrust of up to 200 tons to propel the second stage (a winged rocket named A9) at speeds of up to 2,700 miles per hour and to an altitude of 245 miles. Despite Thiel's death during the *Hydra* raid work continued on the A10 and in 1944 the booster was redesigned, being replaced by an enormous single engine which burned diesel and nitric acid, giving a fifty second burst that produced 375,750lb of thrust.

Though the war ended before these more advanced rocket systems had been finalised, Allied leaders were keen to acquire such technology and as the war in Europe was brought to a close, the race was on by the victorious Allied nations to seize as much of the German technology, and the German scientists, as they could. ●

Notes

1 *The Scotsman*, Thursday, 12 April 1945.
2 Information panel at the Fortress Mimoyecques Museum. For more information, please see: www.mimoyecques.fr
3 Quoted on the Dix Noonan Webb website: www.dnw.co.uk. The casualty figures for the raid vary dramatically, some sources suggesting that the attack led to the death of some 300 Germans and forced labourers. Information panels in the Fortress Mimoyecques Museum, however, state that 'the human loss on the building site seems to have been limited – the archives report two Germans and nine "foreigners" killed'.
4 Information panel at the Fortress Mimoyecques Museum.

The Last to Fall

IT WAS AT THE END OF MARCH 1945, JUST A MATTER OF WEEKS BEFORE THE THIRD REICH'S SURRENDER, THAT THE LAST OF THE V WEAPONS REACHED BRITISH SHORES.

The early hours of Tuesday, 27 March 1945, were little different than any others since the start of Hitler's V weapon campaign. The first V2 to strike that morning did so in Edmonton at 00.22 hours. It was followed by five others, in Cheshunt at 03.02 hours, Ilford at 03.30 hours, Sutton Park at 04.04 hours, Stepney at 07.21 hours, and, finally, in Orpington at 16.54 hours.

The penultimate of these incidents, Big Ben No.1114, was one of the worst ever seen. The V2 fell in the centre of a three-block estate in Vallance Road and the three buildings nearest the impact point, known as Hughes Mansions, were devastated by the blast. In this incident the dead unusually outnumbered the wounded by 134 to forty-three seriously injured.

The by now highly efficient civil defence services were still hard at work in and around Vallance Road when the distinctive double-bang of a V2 explosion echoed out across the streets of Orpington in Kent, the missile having struck the ground in the back gardens between Court Road and Kynaston Road. It blasted a crater forty feet across

BELOW *One that got through – a V1 flying bomb in the last few seconds of its flight before it fell on to the streets and buildings of London somewhere in the vicinity of Piccadilly station.* (HISTORIC MILITARY PRESS)

and twenty feet deep, with people reporting feeling and hearing the explosion for miles around.

A number of residents had lucky escapes. A Police Inspector was resting at his home at No.69 Court Road, listening to a radio programme about the imminent end of the war in Europe, when his ceiling and roof fell in on him. Two children in the garden of No.96 Kynaston Road were saved as they had been playing inside an Anderson Shelter at the time. In total, however, twenty-three people from both roads were seriously injured.

Thirty-four-year-old Ivy Millichamp was standing in the kitchen of her home at No.88 Kynaston Road; she caught the full force of the blast. Her husband Eric, who had been asleep in the front room, survived the explosion and managed to pull his wife from the wreckage, only to find that she was dead.

A month later, on 26 April, Ivy's sister, Mollie, wrote to their father after a speech by Winston Churchill in which he recorded that the threat from the V2 had finally passed. 'How poignant such a statement comes home to us,' she said, 'yet we are only one family amongst many thousands who have suffered in a worse degree. Ivy's face, as Ernie and I saw it, often recurs to my mind. There is however one consolation. I feel she suffered no pain; death must have been instantaneous.'[1]

German records show that by 7 April 1945, they had successfully launched 1,190 V2s against London, of which 163 failed during or shortly after launch. Of the successful

launches, the fall of 1,115 was detected, and of these 518 fell in the London Civil Defence Region.[2] It should be remembered that civilians all over Europe suffered equally badly. Antwerp, a vital port for the Allies, was, for example, the target of 1,610 rockets and 8,696 flying bombs.

Ivy Millichamp was the last civilian killed in Britain as a result of enemy action during the Second World War. The V2 that killed her was the last to reach the UK. However, it was not the end of the V weapon campaign.

ABOVE *A view of the rebuilt Hughes Mansions in Vallance Road, Stepney. Note the memorial to the events of 27 March 1945 that can be seen in the foreground by the trees.* (COURTESY OF ROBERT MITCHELL)

The final Doodlebugs

Whilst the rockets had continued to arrive throughout the first three months of 1945, the last V1 over the UK had been reported on 14 January. Over the weeks that followed there had been no sign of a resumption of air-launched flying bombs attacks, which were the only means of attacking the United Kingdom unless the Germans increased the range of the flying bomb beyond the 130 miles which had so far been the limit of its operations. However, evidence ▶

LEFT *The memorial to the victims of the Hughes Mansions V2 incident on 27 March 1945.* (COURTESY OF ROBERT MITCHELL)

RIGHT *The headstone marking the last resting place of Ivy Millichamp. Ivy was originally laid to rest in an unmarked grave in All Saints Churchyard on 3 April 1945. As the inscription on the headstone states, she was the last civilian killed in the UK through enemy action in the Second World War.* (HISTORIC MILITARY PRESS)

began to accumulate in February 1945 that this was precisely what the enemy was attempting to do.

It appeared that by reducing the weight of the wing of the V1, by using a large proportion of wood instead of steel in its construction, and perhaps also the weight of the warhead by replacing the usual steel casing with wood, the amount of fuel that could be carried, and therefore the endurance and range of the bomb, had been increased. Wreckage that was recovered in February from flying bombs that had crashed in Belgium indicated that such alterations had been embodied in production models.

The predictions of a new wave of flying bomb attacks were proven correct on 3 March 1945. The first V1 reported that day penetrated the defences and fell in Bermondsey at 03.01 hours. Six more were reported in the next three hours, followed by a lull until the middle of the afternoon. Then, from 14.30 hours until 22.30 hours, seven more bombs were plotted. Of the first twenty-one V1s in this new mini-campaign, seven penetrated to London and exploded there, and ten were shot down by anti-aircraft fire. From the evening of 5 March until the early afternoon of the 29th, a total of 104 flying bombs were plotted.

The last flying bombs to fall in London exploded at 07.54 hours and 07.55 hours on 28 March, at Chislehurst and Waltham Holy Cross respectively. The last to fall anywhere in the United Kingdom was shot down by anti-aircraft fire and fell at Iwade, near Sittingbourne, Kent, at 09.59 hours on 29 March. The last to approach the coast was also brought down by anti-aircraft fire, off Orfordness, at 12.43 hours that same day. The shooting down of this missile marked the final end of Hitler's much-vaunted V weapon campaign.

A missed opportunity

As one official history noted, the 'last flurry of flying bomb activity against London during March was clearly a failure. It is hard to see in it any serious military purpose, other than the testing of a modified type of flying bomb. It did not divert any Allied forces, other than a single Mustang squadron, from the offensive against Germany: such forces as were used against it were part of the air defences of Great Britain and would have continued in that role whether or not flying bomb attacks had been launched.'

In retrospect, it became clear that the entire V weapon campaign was scant reward for the enormous effort and cost which Dornberger's teams had put into the hugely ambitious project. In some regards, Hitler's instinct that the rocket would play no effective part in the war was correct and if the resources committed to the rockets had been spent on more fighter aircraft, the Allied bombing campaign against Germany might have been blunted. On the other hand, if he had backed the rocket programme with all the funding Dornberger required from the outset, they might just have

BELOW *A view of 88 Kynaston Road, Orpington, Kent (the left-hand half of the building) which was hit by a V2 rocket at 16.54 hours on 27 March 1945. This was the last V2 to hit the UK in the Second World War.* (HISTORIC MILITARY PRESS)

wreaked the vengeance of which the Führer dreamed.

Rodrick Hill, the man who led the campaign against the V weapons, believed that the Germans would have been far better served by concentrating their efforts on strengthening their air force. This was because by the time the Germans were building their launch areas and then firing their missiles, the Allies had achieved air superiority over the skies of Western Europe. It really did not matter how inventive the new weapons were, with the Allies in control of the airspace, the Germans were never going to be able to produce or fire enough of them to make any telling difference to the outcome of the war – because their factories and launch sites had been bombed into oblivion. ●

NOTES

1   Ramsey, Winston G, *The Blitz Then and Now Volume 3* (Battle of Britain Prints International Limited, London, 1987).

2   Ian Jones MBE, *London: Bombed, Blitzed and Blown Up* (Frontline Books, Barnsley, 2016).

To the Stars

THOUGH DORNBERGER AND VON BRAUN KNEW THEY WERE PRODUCING WEAPONS OF WAR, THEY WERE ALSO WELL AWARE OF THE GREAT POTENTIAL THEIR ROCKETS HAD FOR THE EXPLORATION OF SPACE.

ABOVE *Wernher von Braun, with his arm in a cast, and other German scientists pictured with personnel from the US 44th Infantry Division at the time of their surrender in May 1945.* (NARA)

Though Hitler's Vengeance weapons may have had no influence on the outcome of the war, British, Soviet and American leaders had taken careful note of their potential and were all equally keen to acquire the technology and the expertise of the German scientists. While active operations were still taking place the Supreme Headquarters Allied Expeditionary Force (SHAEF) had ordered that all V1 aircraft and V2 rockets that were taken as the Allies overran the launch, assembly and manufacturing sites were to be protected and preserved for analysis and removal back to the UK and the USA.

Similarly, von Braun and 125 of his team wanted to carry on their research but had no desire to fall into the hands of the Soviets. So, in January 1945, as the Third Reich began to crumble, von Braun made plans to move his personnel south from Peenemünde with the intention of giving themselves up to American troops in Austria. Unknown to von Braun he had escaped just in time as Hitler had ordered the execution of him and his team to prevent their capture by the Allies. On 2 May 1945, von Braun and his rocket team surrendered to the US 44th Infantry Division.

That same month, with the war in Europe scarcely over, General Eisenhower ordered the carrying out of test firing of V2 rockets, pointing out that successful trials would save many years of development work by Allied researchers. That such weapons were to dominate the future nature of warfare was already abundantly apparent.

Following the disbanding of SHAEF in the summer of 1945, the further investigation into the rockets fell in part to the War Office, which established the Special Projectiles Operations Group to organise the testing. On 5 June the project was given the name Operation *Backfire*. In order to be able to continue such work, it was necessary to find sufficient examples - it was hoped that thirty complete rockets could be found. The task of tracking them down was handed to Target Force, ▶

RIGHT V2s pictured in the repair facility at Kleinbodungen, Germany, which was captured by tanks and infantry of the US 83rd Armored Reconnaissance Battalion on 10 April 1945. (NARA)

TOP RIGHT A V2 rocket being fired by British personnel, with German assistance, from a launch pad near Cuxhaven in Germany during Operation Backfire, October 1945. (© CROWN COPYRIGHT, 1946)

BELOW A group of 104 German rocket scientists, mostly Peenemünde veterans and including von Braun, pictured at Fort Bliss, Texas, in 1945. The group had subdivided into two sections: a smaller one at White Sands Proving Grounds for test launches and the larger at Fort Bliss for research. (NASA)

more commonly known as simply T-Force, units of which had already been undertaking their prescribed role, which was to 'identify, secure, guard and exploit valuable and special information, including documents, equipment and persons of value to the Allied armies'.

Orders went out to the Allied Army Groups that all V2 components in Germany were to be 'frozen', which ensured that nothing could be evacuated, moved or destroyed. In the British 21st Army Group's sphere of operations large numbers of rocket components were discovered around the towns of Celle and Fallingbostel. These and other parts, large and small, were collected and transported to the Krupps testing ground near Cuxhaven. Some of the components were provided by the US military, drawn from the material they captured at the Mittelbau-Dora concentration camp near Nordhausen. Such was the scale of the operation that some 400 railway cars and seventy Lancaster flights were required to transport 250,000 parts and sixty specialized vehicles to Cuxhaven.

It was not only parts that those conducting the rocket firing tests needed, they also required fuel. One of the individuals seconded to T-Force was Major George Lambert, who recalled the importance of the fuel being shown in a demonstration by von Braun at Kiel in the summer of 1945: 'I was taken to a Scientific Building and in one of the labs, Wernher von Braun gave us a demonstration of one of his famous rocket fuels. He had a beaker containing what he called X stuff, and another beaker containing what he called Y stuff. When he mixed X and Y there was a loud explosion and a shattering of glass. At that time, I had no idea who von Braun was and what a high reputation he had as a rocket-man, or how much damage he had done to England with the ... V2.'[1]

Operation Paperclip

In the end, only three test launches of the rockets were undertaken at

> "I was taken to a Scientific Building and in one of the labs, Wernher von Braun gave us a demonstration of one of his famous rocket fuels. He had a beaker containing what he called X stuff, and another beaker containing what he called Y stuff."

Cuxhaven, but in Operation *Paperclip* the US Army took von Braun's team, which numbered more than 1,600 German scientists, engineers, and technicians, along with all the captured missiles and spare parts that they could find, to Wright Field Air Force Base in the autumn of 1945. Dornberger was of no value to the Americans and he was turned over to the British, being tried, but acquitted, of war crimes for the V2 bombardment of Britain.

The UK also persuaded a smaller number of German scientists to move to Britain. The motive for this was partly explained in a Foreign Office report: 'It has hitherto been an objective of British policy to encourage the smaller powers, particularly in Europe, to equip their forces with aircraft and weapons of British design. If these countries were to obtain technical reinforcement by recruitment of German research workers and designers, they would be

less likely ... to rely upon armaments of British design.'[2]

The initial driver for the Americans was the aim of putting satellites into orbit for reconnaissance – particularly to monitor the activities of America's new enemy, the Soviet Union. The scientific value of such endeavours was not ignored, however, and at the Army Ordnance Proving Ground at White Sands, deep in the desert country of southern New Mexico, the German technicians worked alongside American officers and field crews in putting reassembled V2s to use for research. As replacing the explosive in the warhead with scientific instruments and ballast would permit observing and recording data on the upper atmosphere, the Army invited other government agencies and universities to share in making high-altitude measurements by this means. The Germans, headed by von Braun, and the General Electric Company, under a contract with the Army, took charge of the launchings, and from laboratories of the armed services designed and built

ABOVE LEFT
A captured V2 rocket is prepared for firing by Allied personnel, almost certainly during the tests at Cuxhaven. (NARA)

ABOVE RIGHT *A V2 captured by the Russians being transported to the Kapustin Yar Test Site. This particular V2 was launched on 18 October 1947.* (MINISTRY OF DEFENCE OF THE RUSSIAN FEDERATION)

BELOW *A captured V2 pictured at Hamburg, bound for the UK, during 1945/46. The rocket has been identified as being the one on display today at the RAF Museum, Cosford.* (HISTORIC MILITARY PRESS)

the instruments placed in the rockets' noses. In the course of the next five years, teams from each of the three military services and the universities assembled information from successful launchings of forty instrumented V2s.

As successive launches set higher altitude records, the US Army's *Bumper* project produced and successfully flew a two-stage rocket consisting of a 'WAC Corporal' missile superimposed on a V2. The US Navy, for its part, was not to be left behind. Four months before the Army Ordnance department started work on captured V2s, the Navy Bureau of Aeronautics had initiated a more ambitious research scheme with the appointment of a Committee for Evaluating the Feasibility of Space Rocketry – unmistakably inspired by the ideas of members of the Navy intelligence team which had investigated German capabilities in rocketry during the war.

By 22 October 1945, the committee had drafted recommendations urging the Bureau of Aeronautics to sponsor an experimental program to devise an earth-orbiting 'space ship' launched by a single-stage rocket, propelled by

liquid hydrogen and liquid oxygen, and carrying electronic equipment that could collect and transmit back to earth scientific information about the upper atmosphere. As a result, the newly organised Rocket-Sonde Research Section of the Naval Research Laboratory (NRL) decided that because the supply of V2s would not last indefinitely, that a new rocket should be built expressly for research.

Meanwhile, a number of groups of scientists and mathematicians declared that the technology that had already been devised was equal to the task of launching a spaceship. The ship could be circling the earth, they averred, within five years – namely by mid-1951. They admitted that it could not be used as a carrier for an atomic bomb and would have no direct function as a weapon, but they stressed the advantages that would nevertheless accrue from putting an artificial satellite into orbit. It was argued, having successfully acquired von Braun's team and so much of their equipment, that 'the consternation ... that would be felt here, if the United States were to discover suddenly that some other nation had already ▶

put up a successful satellite', would be immense. That other nation was, of course, the Soviet Union. Such arguments, surprisingly, failed to win the day, and the US Army and US Navy continued with their own schemes. Part of the reason for this was that the initial velocity required for launching an intercontinental rocket missile would be 4.4 miles per second, while a satellite requires 5.4 miles per second. The dissipation of effort was compounded when the US Air Force split from the Army and began its own space programme. It also meant that funding for the respective space programmes was extremely limited with von Braun remarking that 'at Peenemünde we had been coddled, here you were counting pennies'.

The Redstone rocket

In 1949 von Braun's team launched an Army Bumper-WAC, once again a marriage of a WAC-Corporal missile sitting atop a German-made V2, which achieved a record-breaking flight to an altitude of 244 miles, thereby becoming the first human-made object to enter space.[3]

During much of this period, von Braun and his fellow German scientists were held at Fort Bliss in circumstances similar to house arrest, but as memories of the war faded and the Korean War began, their situation became more relaxed and in 1950 Braun and his German colleagues were moved to Huntsville, Alabama, and allowed to live a more normal life.

Between 1952 and 1956, von Braun led the US Army's rocket development team at Redstone Arsenal, resulting in the Redstone rocket, which was used for the first live nuclear ballistic missile tests conducted by the United States.

It was in 1952 that a series of articles written by von Braun in three issues of *Collier's* magazine sparked the imagination of the American public. His articles chiefly stressed the exciting discoveries that were possible. 'Ten to fifteen years from now, depending on how determinedly and efficiently we shall respond to this challenge,' he wrote, 'the earth will have a second satellite, a man-made moon circling the earth at an altitude of slightly more than 1,000 miles in two hours. Assembled from prefabricated parts hauled into the orbit by huge, three stage rocket ships of the weight of a light cruiser, this station will probably have the shape of a huge wheel of some 250 feet in diameter. It will slowly rotate about its hub and its 80 to 100 inhabitants will live in the wheel's rim.'[4] From

this earth-circling space station American rocket ships could depart to other planets and return, von Braun concluded. No longer were such concepts the stuff of science fiction.

While he was keen to portray the space station as a springboard to man's further ventures into outer space, to the moon and the nearer planets, he added that it would only become a reality because of its tremendous potentialities as a deterrent of war: 'With its powerful telescopic cameras and radar scopes, the station's reconnaissance teams could take the most detailed pictures of any suspect area on the face of the globe at least once every 24 hours. They can thus pull up any Iron Curtain, no matter where they lower it. But while we may well hope that the stations mere existence would seriously discourage any large-scale military adventures, it has far greater potentialities. When it comes down to cases, the station is also a launching platform for orbital guided missiles against which there cannot well be countermeasures.' Just as von Braun's research had been funded by the German Army, thus he now was funded by that of the United States and he had to satisfy his paymasters.

The space platform was for the future, albeit a foreseeable one, but von Braun's more immediate concerns were with using the Redstone rocket to place

a small satellite in orbit. Redstone, a direct descendant of the V2, was sixty-nine feet long, seventy inches in diameter, and weighed 61,000lbs. Its power plant used liquid oxygen as an oxidizer and an alcohol-water mixture as fuel. A new Redstone engine built by the Rocketdyne Division of North American Aviation Inc., and tested in 1953, was 30 per cent lighter and 34 per cent more powerful than that of the V2.

Funding for the satellite project was a major issue until, at last, the US Army and US Navy finally came together. The upshot was an agreement that the Army should design and construct the booster system, while the Navy take responsibility for the satellite, tracking facilities, and the acquisition and analysis of data. Further support came in 1953 from President Eisenhower who announced that, in contrast to the $100 million spent in 1940 on federal support of research and development, he was submitting a $2 billion research and development budget to Congress for the 1955 financial year, with a considerable portion being allocated to the space program.

This was, no doubt, prompted, at least in part, by claims made in November 1953 by the Soviet Academy of Sciences that satellite launchings and moon shots were already feasible. This was followed in March 1954 with Moscow Radio exhorting Soviet youth to prepare for space exploration, and, in April, the Moscow Air Club announced that studies in interplanetary flight were beginning.

In his 1952 magazine articles, von Braun had also visualised sending a spaceship to the moon. 'The first trip to the moon will not involve a landing thereon,' he had stated. 'It will rather be a trip around the moon which will enable the ship's crew to take – for the first time – a glimpse at the unknown back side of the moon. But man's exploring urge will not rest before the first explorers have actually set foot upon the moon's surface.' This would soon become the overriding aim of the United States' space programme. The US, though, was stunned by the launch in 1957 of the first artificial earth satellite by the Soviet Union.

A giant leap for mankind

On 4 October 1957, Sputnik 1, the first artificial Earth satellite, was launched into orbit. Travelling at 18,000 miles per hour it circled the earth for three weeks. The response to this across America was both fear that the Russians were able to threaten the US from space and embarrassment that the Communists had outstripped the champions of democracy in technical proficiency. But at least, from von Braun's point of view, funding was no longer an issue.

Consequently, on 31 January 1958, nearly four months after the launch of Sputnik 1, von Braun and the United States successfully launched its first satellite on a four-stage Juno I rocket, ▶

ABOVE *The remains of a V2 rocket being recovered from salt marshes on the east seawall of Wallsea Island, Essex, in March 2012. The badly split and twisted combustion chamber is believed to be from an air-burst that occurred over nearby Foulness.* (COURTESY OF JOHN MYERS; WWW. GEOGRAPH.ORG.UK)

ABOVE LEFT *A view of the V2 combustion chamber from the Wallsea Island recovery showing the damage caused by the premature detonation of the warhead at altitude.* (COURTESY OF JOHN MYERS; WWW. GEOGRAPH.ORG.UK)

which in turn was derived from the US Army's Redstone missile, at Cape Canaveral. The Space Race had begun.

On 29 July 1958, the National Aeronautics and Space Administration, almost universally referred to as NASA, was formed. Two years later, NASA opened the Marshall Space Flight Center at Redstone, and the Army Ballistic Missile Agency's development team, led by von Braun, was transferred there. Von Braun became the centre's first director, a post he held until 27 January 1970 – by which time man had stepped onto the moon.

The rocket which propelled Apollo 11 to the moon was von Braun's brainchild. This was the Saturn rocket which was effectively an advanced and more powerful A4. This, though, was a three-stage vehicle with liquid oxygen as the oxidizer to a refined petroleum propellant powering the first stage, and liquid hydrogen for the second and third stages.

It was the fifth generation of this rocket, Saturn V, which, on 16 July 1969, shot Armstrong, Aldrin and Collins on their historic journey to the moon. ●

NOTES

1 Quoted in Sean Longdon, *T-Force, The Race for Nazi War Secrets*, 1945 (Constable, London, 2009), p.225.

2 Quoted in the *Guardian* 29 August 2007.

3 For more information see www.nasa.gov.

4 *Collier's* magazine, 22 March 1952.